SO-AYX-079

Then the Rain Came

One Woman's Discovery of God's
Blessings During a Financial Meltdown

Jami Tadda

PRESS

Copyright © 2011 by Jami Tadda

Then the Rain Came
by Jami Tadda

Printed in the United States of America

ISBN 9781613790649

All rights reserved solely by the author. The author guarantees all contents are original and do not infringe upon the legal rights of any other person or work. No part of this book may be reproduced in any form without the permission of the author. The views expressed in this book are not necessarily those of the publisher.

Unless otherwise indicated, Bible quotations are taken from The HOLY BIBLE, NEW INTERNATIONAL VERSION®. Copyright © 1973, 1978, 1984 by International Bible Society. Used by permission of Zonderdervan Publishing House; The King James Version of the Bible (KJV); The New King James Version (NKJV). Copyright © 1982 by Thomas Nelson, Inc. Used by permission; and *The Living Bible* (TLB). Copyright © 1971 by Tyndale House Publishers, Inc. Used by permission.

www.xulonpress.com

This book is dedicated to my fellow travelers on this journey called life. It is my earnest prayer that something on these pages would encourage you and point you towards Jesus Christ, our everlasting hope. Hold on to His promises, and know that He will help you to overcome and live a victorious life in spite of external circumstances.

My deepest and most heartfelt prayer is for those of you who do not yet know Jesus Christ as their personal Lord and Savior. I pray that you would make that eternal decision today and begin to develop a relationship with the awesome Creator of the universe. He intimately knows you—your name, your past, and your present struggles. He cares deeply for you and has already forgiven all your sins. Reach out to Him, accept His love, and know that He promises to never let go of your hand.

CONTENTS

Preface

This book tells the story of my tumultuous journey through the wilderness of financial devastation. It is a journey that includes the loss of material wealth and ends with a deeper awareness and appreciation of God's presence in my life. It is a story of how, despite losing the riches I had, I became richer than ever before. Let me explain.

We all go through tough times, a wilderness of sorts. It is a part of life. You see, it is not *if* we will walk in the wilderness, but *when*. Sometimes our wilderness journey is due to health issues, loss of a loved one, marital problems, trouble with children, aging parents, or, as in my story, financial demise. But regardless of the specific trial, these times of hardship have the ability to bring us to a deeper level of understanding of both ourselves and the God we serve. Oftentimes, after much reflection, we can recognize the blessings that God has given to us in the trial and how much we have grown as a result.

After twenty years of living in Arizona, I have come to appreciate how precious rain is to the desert.

This precious rain reminds me of God's blessings. New life, new growth, and new beginnings occur only after the rain. But oftentimes the refreshing desert rain is preceded by a monsoon storm.

Typically, Arizona monsoon storms start with heavy winds that cause a visible wall of dust hundreds of feet high to move across the valley. These dust storms, or haboobs, are normally accompanied by frequent thunder and lightning and heavy downpours. Sometimes the trees are damaged and flash flooding rearranges the landscape. In the aftermath, the desert looks broken and abandoned. But then, shortly after the storm passes, the cacti begin to bloom. The desert becomes a kaleidoscope of color and life that without the terrible storms would have remained hidden.

God promises us His blessing in John 1:16: "From the fullness of His grace we have all received one blessing after another." He promises this yet again in Ezekiel 34:26: "I will send down showers in season; there will be showers of blessings." However, at times we get so caught up in the problems and difficulties of life that pour down like torrential monsoons that we miss God's gentle blessings. Yet, if we have eyes to see, we can discover the grandeur, beauty, and power of God in our lives, much like we witness the desert in bloom after the storm.

This is my wilderness account and the blessings God used to mark my trail as He showed His love and encouragement to me. I have used my personal journal entries to help me recall the events and used its dates as headings in this book to chronicle my progress.

God did not show me favor because I go to church, because of my profession of faith, or because of any other aspect of *me*. He displays His works because of His grace and for His glory and His glory alone. I have always known this truth, but to fully appreciate that knowledge in my heart as well as in my head took some time. The road to that realization has been exciting, stressful, and adventurous. It has also been more draining and more fulfilling than I could ever have imagined.

My life is truly blessed. I have everything, absolutely everything, I need, and God has given it all to me. I take credit for nothing. My talents, hard work, and perseverance mean nothing and are less than a grain of sand in the sandpainting of my life.

My prayer is that you, too, will be encouraged during your own wilderness journey as you focus on God and refuse to be defined by the storms of life. I pray that you will uncover and identify all the ways that Almighty God, Jehovah-Jireh, "The Lord Who Provides," has blessed you. May the rain of His love always cause you to flourish and bloom as you walk through your own wilderness experience!

Acknowledgments

There are so many people that I desire to thank for their support, love, and assistance to me, not only during my journey through the wilderness, but also afterwards with the completion of this manuscript.

First, I want to give heartfelt praise and thanksgiving to the Lord for His never-ending love and for allowing me to travel through this wilderness. Without the wilderness, I would not be the person I am today. All the glory goes to Him.

To my husband, Kim, who has been beside me each step of the way, you never left, never complained, and never thought less of me. You always give me the support, freedom, and love that I need. I will respect you forever as I am so in love with you. I am blessed to have you as such a wonderful, faithful husband. We truly have something special. Thank you for not only your love and insights, but also for reading the first manuscript and helping determine its final title. May God continue to show Himself to you and hold you close in the palm of His hand.

To my parents, Jack and Theda, who have always been my biggest supporters, you taught me of God and His love through word and action. You provided me with a blessed childhood and gave me the truly wonderful gift of *family*. You have shown me the way I should always go, and I would be wise to follow in your footsteps. I am forever grateful for you. May God continue to shower blessings upon you both. I love you.

To my brothers, Jeff and Troy, two of my best friends, I am so grateful that we remain so close. No matter what life brings, we are always there for each other. I do not take this gift or either of you for granted. I pray God's richest blessings on you both. Thank you for being the first to read this manuscript and for your insights. Jeff, thank you for your assistance, and Troy, many thanks for suggesting the final title.

To my two sisters-in-law, Judi and Teresa. I am honored to call you *family*. May you be encouraged in your walks with the Lord. Remember, He knows your name and loves you deeply and unconditionally. May each of you always hear His still, small voice. May our love and bond continue to grow.

To my friends, Robin, Tammy, Lynette, Irene, and Monica, thank you for your friendship, teaching, prayers, and laughter. Laughter is good medicine for the soul, and you gave me many good doses. I cherish and love each of you. An extra thank you goes to Monica and her red marking pen. I never knew there could be so many missing commas in one manuscript. You truly are the comma queen!

To my friend Nancy, of all the people in my life, you were the one in the trenches with me on a daily basis. Together we worked on how to creatively buy houses, find tenants, evict tenants, strip wallpaper, rezone commercial land, and figured out endless amounts of paperwork. Together, we cleaned toilets and even got scammed by so-called professionals. Real estate brought us together, but our mutual respect, encouragement, and trust built a friendship that will last a lifetime. We have been through a lot of life together; thank you for being in the fire with me. I admire all that you have done and accomplished since I met you eight years ago. You are the sister I never had. May God richly shower you with His blessings!

Finally, I want to thank Brenda for all of her editing. You took a manuscript with many threads and helped weave it all together. I appreciate your expertise and professionalism very much. May God bless you as you assist His people.

1

Year 2000: The Beginning

The year 2000 found me working for a small company in Phoenix, Arizona. I had been there for ten years and had enjoyed working in a number of different departments. Basically, life was pretty good.

The previous year, 1999, I had been transferred to the sales department. It was not a position I would have applied for myself, but one that was thrust upon me by management. I knew I was out of my league, but I also knew that God would provide the sale orders that I needed in order to be successful.

Many years ago when I first left home, my mom shared a wonderful secret with me. She told me that whenever I felt like I needed something solid to hold on to, I should select a Bible verse that fit the situation and memorize it. Then, when I needed a reminder that I was not alone and that God was looking out for me, I could recite or read His promise to me. Her advice gave me great comfort, and over the years I shared this secret with many others.

At this time in my life, in the year 2000, I chose 1 Chronicles 29:11–12 as my personal Scripture verse: "Everything in the heavens and earth is yours, O Lord, and this is your kingdom. We adore you as being in control of everything. Riches and honor come from you alone, and you are the Ruler of all mankind; your hand controls power and might, and it is at your discretion that men are made great and given strength" (TLB). I attached this verse to my appointment book to remind me that if I were to be successful, it would be only because God allowed me to be. I am nothing without Him. And wow, He certainly allowed it! Talk about blessings! I was Rookie of the Year my first year in sales and then made President's Club every year afterward. God abundantly blessed me, and financially I had arrived. I was prospering, well into a six-figure income! Thank You, God!

2

Year 2001: Hold On

I was still doing well and maintaining good sales numbers, but the company was really struggling. As a result, things were very stressful at work. People were on edge and afraid of losing their jobs. It seemed as if people were being laid off every week. Salespeople were asked to produce more orders, but less was being delivered. I really wanted to leave but needed the paycheck. My husband had been downsized earlier in the year, and we were in the process of building our new home.

On September 11, 2001, I was on a client call in Washington, D.C., five miles from the Pentagon. That day, as it did for so many others, prompted major changes in my life. Rather than relive the whole thing, it might be easier for me to share with you a presentation I wrote for a small senior group on the first-year anniversary of the attack. Even though the talk took place a full year later, my feelings and emotions were just as fresh as they had been on that terrible day.

Unknown to me at the time, my life path was winding towards the wilderness.

<u>3</u>

<u>Year 2002: Reflections</u>

September 11 — A Year and a Lifetime Later

First, I want to thank you for the opportunity to meet with you. For those who do not know me, I am Jack and Theda's daughter. I am here at the request of Jesus—I really mean that. One morning back in July, I just had the thought that I needed to share my experience with you, though it is quite out of the ordinary for me to do this.

As way of background so that you will have some sense of where I am coming from, let me share a few facts with you:

- I was raised in a Christian family and accepted Christ at the age of twelve. At times I struggle with my walk of faith.
- I hate change. I have been working on accepting it better, but change is not my idea of fun.

- I was so quiet and shy as a child that when we moved and I started at a new high school, my parents and the school staff arranged for me to have someone to sit with at lunch.
- At one time, I desired to marry a minister and join him in full-time ministry. Seven years ago, I married Kim, a wonderful man whose personal relationship with Christ I am uncertain of.
- I have never lived without a phone. It is as much a part of my life as food and shelter.
- Financially minded, I know where every penny in my life comes from as well as where every penny goes. I love budgets and savings.

Now let me share my story by taking you back in time with me to the days preceding and leading up to that fateful day in September when my life changed forever. This is my account of what happened and my thoughts and observations as it was unfolding.

Friday, July 13, 2001

It is my birthday, and I am celebrating eleven years with a company here in Phoenix. I receive the Bible power verse for the day from the radio station KLOVE. It is one of my favorite verses. I have this one committed to memory and have it hanging on the wall behind my PC: "For I know the plans I have for you," declares the Lord, "plans to prosper you and not to harm you, plans to give you hope and a future" (Jer. 29:11).

Great! This was very encouraging, particularly since my career is in the uncertainty of sales. I know with all my heart that God is the only reason I am successful in any position, but I think this job is one where I especially need to depend on Him a lot. Nevertheless, He has blessed me abundantly. (Sales is a pretty big step for someone who was afraid to make a friend for lunch. See, God really does do miracles!)

My brother Troy gave me a CD for my birthday, titled *Mercy Project*. One song, "You Will Get Through This," is rather catchy. Little did I know how important this catchy little tune would later prove to be.

Without my knowing or understanding, the groundwork for the battle ahead was being laid. Change was in the air, and God was about to reveal Himself with power, glory, and might.

Monday, July 16

My boss tells me that the company is really struggling financially and that there are going to be many layoffs, including most of the sales team. He already knows his job has been eliminated, and at some point, I will be let go as well. It is not a normal downsizing of just a few people, but desperate people and desperate companies sometimes do desperate things. This is not new information, but some of the details my boss shares really bring the facts into light. It appears preparations are being made for the company to be sold. *Okay, God, I am going to hang on to my birthday verse.*

Work continued to be very, very stressful. People were being let go every week. The business tactics grew worse, and negative people surrounded me.

Many of my coworkers were bitter; we all feared for our jobs. I began to hate going in each morning.

But despite the difficult surroundings, God continued to bless me. I was one of the few people with any orders. I knew it was not because I was naturally good at sales, because I truly am not. Besides, there were many other seasoned salespeople who had no orders. There was no explanation for my success except that God Himself was blessing me. I thanked Him every day and believed that with His help, I would get through this rough patch in my career.

I listened often to the CD I got for my birthday and soon memorized track 4. Listen to its words:

<u>You Will Get Through This</u> [1]

Pull the shade down on the sun
Don't want to see the morning break another day
I don't have the strength to face

Close the door and keep it shut
Lord, the ache is just too much for me to take
How do I begin to pray

My way back to some kind of peace of mind
But then I hear love whispering through the darkest of times

CHORUS
You'll get through this
You'll break new ground
When you're lost within your weakness
Hope is waiting to be found

You'll get through this
No matter what it takes
I believe in you for heaven's sake
You'll get through this

Verse 2
When doubts start tearing at
The faith deep in you don't be afraid
Just remember what I said
Nothing formed against you will succeed
As long as your heart's turned towards me

Sunday, September 9

I continue to hang on to my verse; God will provide. As I board a plane for a customer meeting in Washington, D.C., many questions fill my mind: *Will I survive the layoffs and remain employed? Will this be my last customer meeting? Where will I look for work if I need to?*

When planning the trip, I initially told Barbara, my travel agent, that I did not need a rental car, since the hotel was located across the street from the meeting place. However, when I land, I have a feeling that I should get a rental car, so I do.

Monday, September 10

We have meetings all day and are scheduled to start at 7:30 on Tuesday morning.

Tuesday, September 11

I check out of the hotel and go to the meeting, happy in knowing that I will be home in Phoenix around midnight. It is going to be a long day, but I do not mind. This is what I do.

We have fifteen people in the meeting, with several others conferenced in via phone. Things are going well. At 8:45, one of the men on the conference line tells us that a plane has hit the World Trade Center. I wonder how much damage was done to that small plane. We continue with our meeting; after all, this is important stuff. Twenty minutes later, the same man tells us that a 737 has hit the second tower.

We realize now this was not an accident—those poor people! Then we hear another plane has just hit the Pentagon. Oh my gosh, that is only five miles away! The phone goes dead. We all reach for our cell phones, but they, too, are of no use. We rush towards the door, where a bank of pay phones sits right outside. First I dial Kim, then my mom, then Barbara— over and over, dialing and dialing, but still no one answers. The pay phones don't seem to be working either.

What is going on? Is this the end? Will this start the rapture? Oh my, what about Kim? My heart is racing, I am sweating, and adrenaline is flowing. Are my loved ones safe? *Kim, oh Kim, please accept Christ!* My frantic prayers are for my family's safety, but even more frantic are my prayers that someone will lead Kim to Christ, if he needs it. Is he or is he not saved? I cannot stand not knowing.

Why didn't I press him more so I knew where he stood? Are planes dropping out of the sky all over? Someone answer the phone! I feel so isolated—so very alone. *God, take care of my family,* I pray yet again.

Finally, I get through to Barbara. She confirms that the two towers have been hit. It looks like one may collapse, she says.

I immediately know I will not be going home this night. I need shelter, so I leave what is left of the meeting and go back to the hotel and check in for two additional nights. I have been stranded before and know how quickly the hotels will fill up and how air travel will be delayed.

I should feel better, knowing that I have a place to stay, but my mind is still on my family. *Is my family safe?* I wonder. *Barbara did not say anything about what was happening in Phoenix, so all must be fine,* I tell myself. Why am I still shaking? I am so alone.

I watch the images from the hotel TV; it is terrible. One last time I try to reach someone in my family, and to my great relief, my mom picks up. I try to be calm, but I do not succeed. "Did you see the news? This is terrible. I am okay for now, and I have a room. Phones are not consistently working, and my cell phone is useless. Please call Kim for me. I love you all. Good-bye, good-bye".

I should get back to the meeting; they will wonder what happened to me since I did not tell anyone that I was going back to the hotel. As I enter the meeting room, everyone is milling around. We agree we need to continue, reasoning that if we stay focused on something, it will help to calm us down. But many of these people had coworkers, friends, and family in both the World Trade Center and the Pentagon. They are visibly worried and shaken. The work does not seem important any longer.

When I first heard the song "I Was There" in church after 9/11, I was struck by how God truly was with every person entrapped in that terrible tragedy and how He offered the promise of eternal life up to their last breath on this earth. God is so gracious and merciful.

Whenever I hear that song, I picture myself with each person, with all of the emotions of that day coursing through my veins. Let me share its words with you:

I Was There [2]

You say you will never forget where you were when you heard the news on September 11, 2001.
Neither will I.

I was on the 110th floor in a smoke filled room with a man who called his wife to say, "Good-bye."
I held his fingers steady as he dialed

I gave him the peace to say, "Honey,
I am not going to make it,
but it is OK...I am ready to go."

I was with his wife when he called, as she fed breakfast to their children.
I held her up as she tried to understand his words and as she realized he wasn't coming home that night.

I was in the stairwell of the 23rd floor when a woman cried out for Me for help. "I have been knocking on the door of your heart for 50 years!" I said, "Of course I will show you the way home - only believe in Me now."

I was at the base of the building with the priest ministering to the injured and devastated souls. I took him home to tend to his flock in heaven. He heard my voice and answered.

I was on four of those planes, in every seat, with every prayer. I was with the crew as they were overtaken. I was in the very hearts of the believers there, comforting and assuring them that their faith has saved them.

I was in Texas, Kansas, London. I was standing next to you when you heard the terrible news.
Did you sense Me?

I want you to know that I saw every face. I knew every name - though not all know Me. Some met me for the first time on the 86th floor.

Some sought Me with their last breath.

Some couldn't hear Me calling to them through the smoke and flames; "Come to Me...this way...take My hand." Some chose, for the final time,
to ignore Me.

But, I was there.

I did not place you in the tower that day. You may not know why, but I do. However, if you were there in that

explosive moment in time, would you have
reached for Me?

September 11, 2001 was not the end of the journey for
you. But someday your journey will end. And I will
be there for you as well. Seek Me now while I may be
found. Then, at any moment, you know you are
"ready to go."

I will be in the stairwell of your final moments.
Remember...I love you

Back to the meeting room: We sit down and try to focus, but it is a hopeless task. I nervously walk out into the hallway, desperately needing to call someone, to reach out to someone. I finally reach Kim. He is physically safe for now. I thank God for that, but my prayers continue to rise on his behalf.

I look out the twenty-first-floor window in the hallway by the pay phones and see men dressed all in black, with facemasks and guns, scaling the building next to ours. I look down into the parking lot, and men are searching through cars, and there are dogs all over. I can hear nothing but the pounding of my heart.

Then I notice more men scaling our building as well. *Are they terrorists? Is this really the end?* my mind screams. Yet I am at peace with God, though this is not the way I thought my life would end. I so desperately want to be with my family. I want to hear them, touch them, and tell them that I love them just one more time.

I go back into the meeting room and tell the group about the men. No one knows why they are there. We venture downstairs, and someone tells us the men are with the FBI. But not until a while later do we learn that they were securing all the buildings that housed unmarked FBI offices, and ours was one of them.

About fifteen to twenty minutes later, we are informed that our building is on the flight path to the White House, and we need to evacuate. As a matter of fact, most of Washington was being evacuated. Several of us return to the hotel, as it was the only place we had to go. Others hurry to pick up their children from school before all of the roads are shut down. Some of the children would learn for the first time that some of their friends and loved ones were not coming home.

The five of us from out of town and staying at the hotel are restless yet try not to show our anxiety. I know they, too, are concerned about their loved ones. What do we do? What should we do? We decide to go to dinner, but there is little conversation. We all feel very alone, even in the company of one another.

Wednesday, September 12

We cannot leave the area. There is a five-mile perimeter around the hotel, and almost everything is closed. Thankfully, a Wal-mart is open. I go and buy a change of clothes. My business suit is shot.

Karen, one of the employees of our client, lives in Texas, but she was at the World Trade Center yesterday for a meeting. She made her way to our hotel so she could ride back to Texas with the rest of her group once the roads open. She is covered in dirt, smoke, and sweat, yet she is a sweet sight to see. We all surround her and bombard her with questions for which she really has no answers. All she knows for sure is that New York is a mess.

Karen spent many hours getting to the hotel, what with the mass of humanity surrounding ground zero. She confirms that all of her team was safe when she left New York and headed for Washington twenty-four hours ago.

Thursday, September 13

Finally! The roads are opened, and they might open the airports later on. But it will be a mess. Planes are all in the wrong cities. Regular service will not be available for several days. Baltimore/Washington International Airport may not open for even longer. No, I am not going to fly; I will take my rental car and drive home. How I thank God that I got the car last Sunday!

I can see the sign for I-70 West from my hotel room, and I know that it takes me home. Several people from Texas offer to caravan with me, but they are going south and that would add twelve hours to my trip. No, it is not worth it, I decide. I need to get west. I need to leave. I need to go home.

Despite my lack of sleep and mental exhaustion, the adrenaline is still flowing. I tell myself to relax so that I can drive. It is 7:00 a.m., and I am heading for the I-70 exit. I did not get a map last night, but it is okay. God will lead me home—through the wilderness.

I drive and drive; I go through Pittsburgh and come close to the site of the fourth plane tragedy. I wonder what happened and how the people felt. I have spent a lot of time flying across this country, and I ponder how I would have felt had I been on that flight.

How do I feel now as I drive across the county? I waffle from feeling sort of numb to having my mind flooded with so many different emotions all at once. I search for information on the radio, anything to help put the pieces together. I see cars driving with American flags stuck to their side windows. I want one too and decide to look for one at the next gas station— anything to feel a sense of belonging. My family and Julie, my coworker, call occasionally to check up on me.

At one point, I realize that I have not seen an I-70 sign for many miles. I must have missed an exit after the last road detour. I call my husband, and we determine that I am headed in the wrong direction. He tells me where I need to turn in order to get back on I-70 West. I am so grateful for him.

At times I can almost hear God speaking to me— assuring me I am okay but that change is coming. Sixteen hours later, I am in St. Louis. I find a hotel in a not-so-good part of town, but I am too tired to look for another place. The night clerk hands me the key, and after a hot shower, I sleep for three hours. By 4:00 a.m., I am ready to hit the road, anxious to continue west. The same night clerk gives me a banana as I check out.

Friday, September 14

I must remember to eat today, but I continue to drive. At times I feel God's presence. Fourteen hours later, I finally make it to Colorado. This is as close to home as I will be for a few days. My brother and sister-in-law live here. They are family, and I will stay with them. That night I sleep for three hours and again wake with the need to keep moving. I cannot seem to stay still. I am driven to keep moving.

Saturday, September 15

I drive to the mountains towards my grandma's house; it is safe there. But when I get there, it is not the same. She had moved to Arizona to live with my parents, and we were in the process of cleaning out her house and selling it to the City of Boulder for a mining museum. So it is empty, and no one is home. There is no coffee, no signs of life. Something else I thought would never change has done just that. Does no one else feel the emptiness of it all? Am I the only one? I am so alone.

My husband drives to Colorado to meet me. When I see his face, I finally break down and cry. I cannot hold back the tears any longer. In his arms, I sleep for five hours that night, but the insane need to keep moving continues to drive me. We finish up the weekend at Grandma's house, and then Kim and I begin the drive home to Phoenix.

We finally reach Arizona, and I see the familiar landscape dotted with cacti. I am home. Yes, I am home, but still I cannot relax.

Kim and I drive to the airport to pick up my car that I had left there nine days earlier. The CD my brother gave me is still in the player. Track 4 does not come on, but track 6 does. As I listen to the words, I have the distinct feeling that this was what God was telling me on my drive across the country. Only this time I hear the message more clearly.

Love Won't Leave You Now [3]

Hey, I can see all your dreams
Lying scattered in your fragile heart
You think your world's come apart

But hey, I believe there's gonna be
A brighter day that shines for you my friend
It's waiting around the bend

You've been dancing on the wire
Walking through the fire
Thinking you are all alone
But you are not on your own

There's been a faithful hand to guide you
God will always be beside you
All because He is love
And love won't leave you now

So fly, on the wings of your dreams
To the places He is taking you
You're gonna make it through

And, if you doubt, just think about
All the promises that He has made
You do not have to be afraid

Through the smiles
Through the sorrow

He was faithful yesterday, and
He'll be faithful tomorrow.

The song soothes my battered heart. *Thank You, God. You were with me the whole time. I knew it; I sensed it. I was alone, but I knew You were close by, protecting me.*

And God had indeed been with me. He provided me with a car and a safe hotel room, and He put understanding people in my path. I was among strangers, and yet they went out of their way to make sure I was taken care of and had a way home. God led me safely across the country despite my lack of sleep. I was kept out of harm's way so many times, so many ways. He answered so many prayers. But then, God's never-ending mercy is always shown best in the worst of times.

But things are far from over. The very next day, my parents and I turn around and drive back to Colorado so we can finish packing Grandma's house. I know it is going to be a very emotional task. But it has to be done, and it has to be done this week.

On the long drive from Phoenix to Boulder, I finally relax a little and have time to think. *God, I know something is happening. I am willing to leave the security of my job, if that is what You want. Do I need to go into ministry? Do I need to witness to people, like I so desperately wanted someone to do for Kim? God, I feel like I am losing everything! My job, our family home, my security—yes, I even thought I had lost Kim. Help me! Lead me! I am so afraid, God—so afraid of change.*

Thoughts like these keep me on edge most of the week, but at times I can hear God assuring me that everything is okay. When I am able to quiet my mind, His peace and a sense of calm sweep over me.

I remember the song I played so much the past few months, the song that said I would get through this, that love would not leave me now. I know in my heart it is true. It is only when my head takes over that I give in to doubt and start to panic.

With all the events of the past three months I knew my life was changing, and no matter how hard I fought to keep it the same, it would never be. My journey had only begun, and I would have to learn to surrender and trust God in a way I had never done before.

My friends, what does this mean for you? Why am I really here today, speaking with you and sharing my story? I think the message is not so much about what happened to me as it is what God can do for and with you.

I know you are all facing your own challenges. You might be afraid, feel all alone, or not see how you can take even one more step. Insurance, health, family, church, and job issues—they all build up. You sometimes feel trapped and so tired of fighting the good fight. But I am here to encourage you today, to tell you that Jesus has not forgotten you. He is right there.

So reach out to Him, ask for His blessing, and hold on to His promises. Find a promise that touches you today and hold on to it. Remember, God has a plan and is working in your life to bring it about. You are not too old to be used by Him.

What about those of you who are being used by God? Don't grow discouraged when it seems like the work is in vain and that the younger generation does not appreciate you. Hang in there every day.

And for those of you who might not know Jesus or have a personal relationship with Him—what about you? Are you going to wait another day to make that eternal decision? Who knows what will happen this afternoon, tomorrow? When will your September 11 come? Are you ready?

If not, I offer you a promise: God will reach out and hold you in His arms if you will just take the first step and ask Him into your life. Do not wait another minute, for tomorrow may not come. It did not for many people in the World Trade Center, in the Pentagon, and on that plane over Pittsburgh on September 11, 2001.

The hand of God continued to work in my life in mighty ways between the events of 9/11 and a year later when I gave this talk to the senior church group. Looking back, I could see God's blessings like raindrops marking my path. Knowing what lay ahead of me, He provided a Scripture verse and a song to encourage me when work was difficult and I was discouraged. He prompted me to get a rental car so that I could leave Washington and drive home. He provided protection both during the attacks and on the drive home. He provided me with a loving husband, family, and friends.

Can you see His hand of provision? Even though I felt out of control and had many different emotions flooding my brain all at once, I now know He had me cradled in His hand, providing exactly what I needed. Can you see His perfect timing in giving me what I needed at just the right time? As I learned, sometimes He stills the storm, and sometimes He stills the child.

Moving into 2002, I believed that God had and continued to have a plan for me. However, I knew that I needed to learn to surrender and trust Him more, which I continued to work on. During 2002, the following events took place:

1. I spoke to my husband about his salvation. He assured me he was saved, but I continued to pray that he would draw ever closer to God and develop a more personal relationship with Jesus.

2. I had the opportunity to build a stronger friendship with my coworker Julie, and through that friendship, I was able to share my faith in God with her.

3. This next one was a real step of faith for me. I finally left my job in June 2002. The company started asking the sales department to do more and more things that I felt were morally and ethically wrong. In addition, my supervisors called me into the office on several occasions and told me that if I did not make my sales numbers, a particular person in the company would be let go. I had worked with many of these people for over ten years, and now I

was personally responsible for not only my livelihood but also that of other employees. Yes, there were times when I did not make my number, and the company kept its word. When those employees were escorted out, I felt like it was my fault. The company's tactic was extremely unfair, but they knew I would do everything I possibly could in order to produce revenue.

The final straw came when one of my respected clients pulled me aside and informed me that the diminishing reputation of the company and their business tactics were being reflected back on me. I knew then I could not stay; my integrity meant more to me than a paycheck. I did not have another job to go to, but I knew it was the right decision, no matter how difficult. Thankfully, my husband supported my decision.

In one of the many miracles in the Bible, Jesus was walking on the sea when one of His disciples, Peter, got out of the fishing boat and walked on the water to Him. For me, the greater miracle of this story was not that Peter walked on the water, but rather that he was able to get out of the boat in the first place. My boat was my job, and it was very, very hard for me to let go and get out of that boat.

So by September 2002, Kim and I had no steady income. But God is faithful and takes care of His children. I received some of my outstanding commissions from my previous job, Kim did some consulting, and we had our savings. Had I been so blessed the previous two years in sales because God knew we would need the money later? I think so.

Typically, I would have worried about using our savings and not knowing when or how we could replenish it. But God amazingly provided me with a peace that truly surpassed all understanding. I knew God would provide. He had done so in the past—like on 9/11—and I knew He would do it again. That is not to say that at times I did not sometimes waver, especially on the days when my old employer would try to entice me back by offering me a huge base salary with full benefits. They called about every ten days.

4. After receiving the last of my outstanding commissions and after all my job prospects had disappeared, I was given the book *The Prayer of Jabez* by Bruce Wilkinson[4]. The book's main premise is based on 1 Chronicles 4:10: "And Jabez called on the God of Israel saying, 'Oh that You would bless me indeed, and enlarge my territory, that Your hand would be with me, and that You would keep me from evil, that I may not cause pain!' So God granted him what he requested" (NKJV).

The book explained that with this simple prayer, Jabez was asking for God's supernatural blessing. In addition, he was asking for his influence, or ministry, to be expanded and for God's hand of provision to be upon him. I decided to start praying this prayer and, like Jabez, to ask for God's favor and for the opportunity and courage to witness more to others.

I was also starting to think more about my financial situation. There would be no more commission checks coming in, and I knew I really needed God's blessing. I could not depend on myself, but fortunately, I was not afraid or too proud to ask that He bless me in abundance.

And bless me He did, although not all the blessings were financial. Just providing me with peace when I started to grow anxious was a wonderful blessing. He also opened my eyes so that I could see opportunities to witness and then gave me the strength and courage I needed to do it. It might be only a sentence or two, but it was a start. My speaking to the senior group was a prime example of my newfound boldness.

Think about this: If I had not already been on edge because of my job situation, would the events of September 11 still have affected me so deeply? I think not. If I had not been so deeply affected, would I have been able to leave my job? I think not. And if I had not left my job and started to learn how to lean on God for His provision, His peace, and His grace, I would not have been equipped for the next stage of my life. His plan was beginning to unfold. Slowly He was showing me that He is ever faithful, ever merciful, and always trustworthy. These are blessings that cannot be bought at any price.

Yes, my life was changed forever on September 11. God got my attention and showed His power in such an awesome way that there was no denying He is Lord and He is in control.

Many of the seniors had encouraged me to continue trusting God and to follow a new path. Wow! I could not have known what an adventure that was going to be. When I went from earning a six-figure income to living off savings, I actually thought that was going to be the hard part of my wilderness journey. But as I said earlier, God's mercy and grace are shown best in the worst of times, and my journey was just beginning.

By October 2002, Kim and I still had a substantial savings account, and I decided that I would like to try my hand at real estate investing. I started to read, meet with people, and learn everything I could about real estate. I explored the option of doing "fix and flips," in which you buy a house under value, fix it up, and then resell it. I thought it was the perfect option for us, since my husband is so handy. If we could do one transaction a month, I figured, we would be set.

Kim and I went and looked at our first house together. In retrospect, this was the worst house I have ever seen, and I have seen some pretty beat-up houses. Everything about this house was wrong. The wiring was on the outside of the walls, there was no flooring in the kitchen, and there was a big hole cut into the slab where the rusty hot water heater was proudly sitting. Most of the plumbing was missing, and the drywall was more gone than not. Knowing that I wanted to do twelve of these in a year, Kim took one look at this house and told me he absolutely did not want to be involved in real estate! As a result, I started exploring other avenues of real estate investing that did not require the use of quite so many hand tools.

I soon met a realtor who worked primarily with investors, and he invited me to a meeting with him and about twenty other people. As I looked around the room, I realized that with the exception of me, everyone else there was a very seasoned, savvy real estate investor. Some of them were connected to state government, while others had been involved in real estate for many years and boasted large portfolios. Regardless of their particular experience, they all seemed to be so much more knowledgeable than I.

We were all gathered there for a "unique opportunity." It was explained to us that a small local builder was struggling financially. The subdivision of approximately 150 planned homes presently had five houses in various stages of completion. The builder was proposing to sell all of the remaining lots to investors at a greatly reduced price. Then, with our construction financing in place, she would complete the homes and sell them on our behalf to retail buyers for the fair-market value. On paper, approximately thirty to fifty thousand dollars would be made on each property. The only catch was that each investor had to buy a minimum of three lots.

New homes seemed a much better option to me than the one I had just seen, so after watching everyone else sign up, I was convinced and decided to move forward. I gave the title company twenty-five thousand dollars earnest money and then, along with the other investors, waited for the homes to be built. Long story short, either the title company or the builder forged our signatures, because all the earnest money was released to the builder, who then promptly disappeared. *What? Was this the unique part of the deal?* I was left shaking my head.

Our investor group pooled our resources, but we were unsuccessful at suing either party. After many months of working on the issue, meeting together as a group, and discussing what we could do, we decided that walking away from further legal action was our best option. Twenty people lost at least twenty-five thousand dollars, plus some shared attorney fees, but there was nothing more we could do.

I had kept my husband informed about the entire situation. After the final meeting, I went home, crushed. I had to tell Kim that we were out twenty-five thousand dollars with absolutely nothing to show for it. My lip trembled as I relayed the bad news. At that moment, my husband walked over and gently put his arms around me, telling me that the money was gone from our account the day I wrote the check, so it was okay and all was not lost. In that moment, I fell in love with him all over again.

So now I was faced with the question of how to make this real estate investing thing work. Was this really a career choice actual people made? If so, why had I never seen it in any college pamphlet or catalog?

I decided that maybe lease options were the way to go.

To that end, I bought a five-thousand-dollar course that included a three-day training camp. Maybe if I followed a course and tried not to re-create the wheel, I would be able to figure it out, I thought. Returning from the training, I was fired up to make this idea work.

The whole idea with lease options is to help both seller and buyer in the purchase of a home. Sometimes the seller cannot or chooses not to sell the property in the traditional manner with a realtor. Perhaps the house needs a lot of work, or perhaps the seller needs to move right away as a result of a job transfer or a family circumstance. It might be that the seller has no equity in the property to pay for commissions and closing costs. Regardless of the particular situation, the motivation is oftentimes not money. Then there are the buyers, good people who, for whatever reason, just cannot obtain a traditional mortgage. Most of the time, their issue is credit related.

As an investor, I either purchase the property at a discount or take over the seller's existing mortgage payments, sort of like an assumable loan. Then I fix up the house and find a buyer. The buyer pays an option fee and basically rents the property for one to two years until his credit improves to the point that he can qualify for a traditional mortgage. Then, at that time, he will buy the property from me for a prede-termined price, and the option payment goes towards the down payment. The lease option provides sev-eral advantages for the buyer, one of which is that it allows him to earn rent credits every month he pays on time. These credits also are applied towards the down payment.

The more I prayed and thought about this course of action, the more I began to see it as a viable way to help others as well as helping myself. I forged ahead and formed my company, Next Step Properties, LLC. I chose the name because I was the "next step" for both sellers and buyers who had very few options in front of them.

As owner, one of the things I started doing was leaving a Christian book in each of the houses as the new tenant-buyer moved in. I was never sure if anyone ever read the books or if they made any impression on anyone until one day when I was getting the keys back from one of the tenants who was moving out. This woman had gone through a divorce and was struggling to make ends meet. When she handed me the keys, she also handed me the book by Max Lucado that I had left there two years earlier. I could tell the book had been read several times. I told her that if she wanted to keep the book, she could, and she started to cry. She shared how the book had impacted her life and how grateful she was for it and its message. I knew then that I needed to continue to leave my gift in each home as a small raindrop blessing.

Through the years, I helped over 125 families with the lease-option program.

November 2002

My realtor friend took me out to Buckeye, Arizona, a place where he had many investors buying properties. At that time, Buckeye was an up-and-coming community, with just a few houses along I-10. But the expectation was that it would soon flourish and grow with restaurants, grocery stores, and gas stations.

The price for homes was great. Excited, I soon bought my first new home; actually, I bought three new homes in one weekend. Even more exciting, my realtor already had families approved for the lease-option program, and they moved in as soon as I closed escrow. I felt good knowing I did not have to make any mortgage payments while looking for tenants, and an added bonus was that I had their option payments to help cover my closing costs.

A small spring rain fell gently on me.

4

Year 2003: Keep on Climbing

January 2003

I now had three lease-option properties started and was working on a couple of other transactions. However, at times I would grow anxious, as I had no source of income and none in the foreseeable future; in addition, our savings was slowly slipping away. But I was learning a great deal, and I liked the fact that all the decisions were mine. The income would come, I told myself.

March 8, 2003

On this day, I wrote an e-mail to my parents' pastor, a man I greatly respected. I'm including it here because it provides a look into my thoughts and feelings at this point in my journey:

Hi, Dr. R.,

I hope that things are going well with you and your wife. Mom told me earlier this week that you asked how things were going with me. I appreciate your thoughts, and even though you probably are not that interested, I thought I would write to you. This is definitely more for my benefit than yours, but maybe if I articulate what I am feeling, it will shed some light for me.

I am very thankful for the past nine months. Even though quitting my corporate job was one of the toughest things I have ever done, I still maintain that it was for the right reasons and that God allowed it to happen, just as He allowed me to get the job twelve years earlier. Several times during my career, I wanted to quit and move back to Colorado to help my family more, but the door was always closed. So I feel very confident that the time I spent on the job was the exact number of days God wanted me to be there. I was offered my old job back several times and each time was glad that I turned them down.

During the past nine months, I have learned and explored a whole new industry, real estate, one that I previously had only a very brief exposure to. It has been exciting to stretch my wings and actually explore something of interest to me. In advance, God provided a large savings account, which allowed me this opportunity.

Even on the days when Kim and I were at odds with different aspects of my direction, God stepped in and gave us a workable solution that we both could live with. Basically, I do not involve him in the business as much as I had originally hoped. But he supports me in the fact that he does not stop me or curtail my decisions.

I have the beginning infrastructure for a real-estate investment company. I have a few tools in my bag and a beginning understanding, although very basic, of what I am up against. I do not feel that any of this has been in vain or a waste of time. However, I am beginning to question if I should continue this course of employment on a full-time basis.

I have a couple of rent-to-own houses that gross a total of $240 a month. My monthly expenses are obviously quite a bit more than this. Okay, with the price of gas, my income barely covers that one bill, let alone our living expenses and all the expenses to continue the business. I will not really make any money with the rentals for the next two years, not until the people start to purchase the homes from me.

To be honest, I am starting to feel a sense of panic. Kim's consulting has ended, so we are continuing to drain our savings account. I am thinking that I should get a real job—not a career, per se, but something that will help cover our bills. I would like to find something in the real estate field, thus allowing me to further my education and expand my networking base. I think I could work and still continue my own company.

Now my dilemma: Am I not trusting God to provide and merely panicking because I feel out of control in this situation? My savings account has always provided a safety net, and now that it is being reduced, is my faith being tested in an area that is important to me? Or should I allow God to provide through another source of income? Even Moses had to tap the rock to get the water out of it. But that's probably a moot point, since I have no job prospects anyway.

I used to be able to tithe and give a great deal more money to others than I currently do, and that has me troubled as well. I want to be a good steward with the resources God has provided, and thus far, I feel that I have used what I had wisely. But I am at a stopping point now. A trusted friend of mine told me that God would not have brought me this far just to abandon me and that I should stick with the business and watch God provide my literal daily bread. (Okay, that advice was much better when I gave it to her instead of the other way around!) But does she have a point?

I am not looking for you to have the magic answer, but it was good to share some of my thoughts, even if only in an e-mail. So I guess to answer your question about how I am doing, I would have to say that God and I are wrestling in the dirt a bit as I walk through the desert headed for the promised land. Sometimes I see the pillar of fire leading, and other times I do not. But no matter what, I know that God is there. He knows the plans He has for me, plans to give me a hope and a future. I must just cling to Him.

Thanks for listening,
Jami (the wandering desert pilgrim)

May 2003

A friend of mine, a loan officer, offered to hire me as her assistant. I would be paid per file and would have the opportunity to learn more about the mortgage business. This seemed like a perfect solution, so I immediately signed a six-month contract and praised Jesus with a full heart!

June 2003

My loan officer friend was also the founder of a real-estate investing club. It was a great place to network with other investors and learn new things, and I got deeply involved in the group. I also took every real estate course I could get my hands on. Wanting to lay a firm foundation for my business, I set to work learning about different investing techniques, creative financing, tenant-landlord issues and laws, payroll taxes, accounting, and a myriad of other topics.

November 2003

I had always thought that getting a mortgage was extremely chaotic, but I thought that if I learned what happened behind the scenes, it might make the process easier. It did not. I quickly learned that the entire mortgage business is nothing but chaos. Far too many variables come into play, and nothing is ever consistent. No wonder getting a mortgage is a nightmare for all parties involved!

I decided not to extend my contract with my friend and to instead go to school to get my realtor's license. Thinking I might enjoy this part of real estate much more, I once more found myself thanking God for a new opportunity.

December 2003

My previous employer from when I was in sales continued to call me for about six months after I left the company. They continued asking me to reconsider and come back to work for them. After I kept turning them down, they finally quit calling; however, I thought the door would be open to me if I ever changed my mind.

Many times in those trying days, I yearned for the security of a "real" job with a regular paycheck, so during one of those times, I gave in and called my previous employer. I asked if there were any openings for me, but preferably not in sales. However, much to my surprise and great dismay, because of a series of circumstances beyond my control and even my knowledge, I discovered I was being accused of corporate espionage by the president of the company. After meeting with him to find out what they were talking about, I explained I had no idea that the events in question had taken place, and I had certainly done nothing to diminish the company. The president agreed that it was all a misunderstanding; however, there were no positions open for me at this time, he said.

Several months later, I again inquired of a part-time position with my former employer, hoping to supplement my income while still reserving time for my real estate endeavors. In a very unpleasant manner, I was again accused of corporate espionage and ordered never to call there again—for any reason! My former coworkers were instructed that speaking to me would be at the risk of their own employment. It was all very weird.

When I again got to the bottom of this second allegation, I could see their point of view, but once again all of the events had taken place without my knowledge and even in a completely different state. Knowing that there are no coincidences in life, I took this very strange turn of events as a very tightly closed door from God. I guess He really did not want me going back to my comfort zone!

5

Year 2004: The Mountaintop

Things did get better after I got my real estate license and started assisting other investors in buying properties. I was able to help educate them on the lease-option program and soon had some money coming in to cover my bills. God literally expanded my territory. By July, I owned thirteen properties, and my realtor business had really picked up. The market was starting to boom, and I was riding the wave.

March 4, 2004

All of the men on my husband's paternal side of his family died by age fifty-four with a heart attack. Kim, at this time, was fifty-seven; his family history haunted him. At the end of February and continuing into March, he started to experience some chest discomfort off and on. He thought it was merely indigestion, since it did not hurt. However, on the evening of March 4, right after he went to bed, his arm started to tingle.

I immediately drove Kim to the emergency room, and while they were checking him over, he had a heart attack right there in the ER. They rushed him to surgery and cleared a blocked artery. The doctor told me that if we had not been in the ER, Kim probably would have died that night.

I placed my husband on a prayer chain, for both his recovery and the strength to give up smoking. Kim had smoked a pack a day for forty-plus years, but twenty-four hours after his procedure, he came home, threw away his cigarettes, and has not smoked since. Praise God! It was another wonderful blessing, another refreshing rain shower, in my life.

June 2004

Next Step Properties was now a full-time job on top of my full-time job as a realtor. I had studied about eight different in-depth courses on real estate investing, but I soon realized that there was a lot of stuff not included in those books. One thing they failed to mention was how time consuming many of the related tasks were.

By now it was taking four full workdays a month just to keep up with the paperwork and bills for all the mortgages, HOA statements, rent checks, insurance, taxes, and utilities. And this didn't even include the time it took to find tenants. I never would have guessed that filling properties would be such an intense undertaking.

I understood, of course, that potential tenants might not have great credit; after all, we were in business to give them time to improve it. However, I never would have guessed that so many of them would be so irresponsible. Although I would set up an appointment a day in advance to show a property and call to confirm the appointment a couple of hours before the meeting time, more than 50 percent of the prospective tenants never showed up. Then, even after I got a tenant into a property, things would usually go well for five or six months, but then "life" would happen. It seemed that most of my tenants would get a divorce and no longer be able to make the payment. This scenario happened so often that I joked I must be bad for marriages.

Although I tried to work with my tenants in their different financial situations, often they would just disappear overnight, owing me thousands of dollars. I guess aliens abducted them or something along those lines! After they moved out, I would face another huge job: getting the property ready to rent again. My husband and I would usually fill a good portion of our truck with junk the previous tenants had left behind; then I would clean the house as if it were my own, spending many hours scrubbing it from top to bottom. Often we would need to paint and install new carpet, even though we had already done so only a year earlier. Black for bedrooms and midnight blue for bathrooms must have been the hot paint colors for 2004, but let me tell you, they sure take a lot of primer to cover! But I was convinced that all of this work was worth it, and in the end, this was all going to pay off. In the meantime, I really did feel this program was making a difference in a few peoples' lives, and I was encouraged by that.

August 2004

One of my lenders agreed to meet with each of my tenants individually to review their credit reports. She also agreed to write up an action plan so they could know exactly what to do in order to get their credit in a position to secure a loan. I begged all of my tenants to take advantage of this offer, but to my dismay, I could not persuade anyone to make an appointment. *Why won't they help themselves?* I questioned. There was no catch, no risk, no cost—nothing other than the motivation to improve their situation. I will admit, I was quite discouraged that they could not see the value of the offer.

September 11, 2004

As the year began moving towards its close, I turned reflective and felt the need to let my parents know how appreciative I was of them and their steady influence in my life. Here is what I wrote to them:

Mom and Dad,

As I sit here thinking about the events of the past three years, I am so grateful that you have been such a big part of my life. My life was totally turned upside down three years ago, and only by the grace of God was I brought through to the other side. I truly believe that God's hands have been working to bring me from one path to another.

I have always believed that I received the job here in Phoenix by God's grace and that it would take Him to get me to leave it. I know now that it was His will that I leave that job, even though it was not easy to do. I believe that events, others' actions, and situations all worked together to force me to leave my comfort zone. I had to step out of the boat in order to walk on the water.

But thankfully, I did not have to do this alone. It was your support, encouragement, and love that helped push me out of the boat. It was your unfailing belief in me that gave me the courage to try. Much like everything else I have ever done—flying a plane, moving one thousand miles from my family, starting my own business—it was your never-ending love and support that enabled me to reach for the next level. Your love has given me roots and you have helped me to find my wings. This is one of the greatest gifts a parent can give a child, and you do it unceasingly.

In looking back, I can see I had no idea where I was headed or what was happening; and quite frankly, I was pretty scared. I have come a long way in my wilderness walk. Many times I have wanted to go back to Egypt—to my old job, to what I knew—but that door was not just closed, but nailed shut. I had to keep walking and crawling forward. I know that I complained more than I should have, and for that I am sorry. But my faith was and still is being stretched. It is growing, and I am learning, however slowly, to lean on God for everything. What better reward for righteous parents?

Tonight I am faced with many new questions, faced with knowing there is yet another step, recognizing that though I do not know what that step is, I do know who is leading and know He can be trusted. The song that got me through leaving my job states, "You have been walking in the fire / Dancing on the wire / Thinking you are all alone / But you are not alone / For He is love, and love won't let you go." God did not let me go, and neither did you. I can never thank you enough.

December 2004

I ended the year with twenty-two closed transactions. All the bills were paid, and financially things were pretty good. I was content, engulfed in another gentle winter rain of blessings.

6

Year 2005: Cloudy Skies

As 2005 began, things were going really well. I was very busy with clients, so much so that I hardly had time to buy any more properties for myself. I was working twelve to fourteen hours a day just to keep up with everything. Almost all of my clients were investors, and I helped them purchase properties, educated them on the lease-option program, and helped fill their properties with tenants. It was exciting work, and I was living off adrenaline, and enjoying it. God was really blessing my business, both the investments and the traditional real estate.

March 2005

Many of my clients were buying land, and since I had always thought land was a good investment, I let greed get the best of me. I purchased a five-acre lot in Maricopa, Arizona, which was so far from civilization that it might as well have been on the moon. My husband warned me this was not a good investment, but I did not listen to his advice and bought it anyway.

I also bought a much more desirable one-acre lot in Prescott in a private golf community and convinced my brother and sister-in-law, Jeff and Judi, to go in with me and buy a second lot in the same community. We all had visions of selling the lots in a couple of years for a huge profit.

April 2005

During this time, a number of my family and friends wanted to get involved in the real estate market. We came up with a plan for me to borrow their money, use it for down payments on properties, and then, when the houses sold, return their money with 10 percent interest. This seemed like a good plan to all of us. I ended up receiving a hundred thousand dollars from four individuals.

June 2005

Several of my tenants actually followed through on their lease-option programs and purchased their homes. Their purchase prices had been set prior to the market increase, so they had many thousands of dollars in equity when they bought. I was glad to be a part of their good fortune. I once again saw this work as a blessing to others.

As the market continued to skyrocket, Kim wisely advised me to sell my properties, pointing out that they were not worth what the market was currently paying for them. Though I understood his words, I could not see the next step, or what to do after I sold them. I struggled with the idea of selling a house for $200,000 that I had bought the previous year for $125,000, just to turn around and pay $200,000 for its replacement. The thought of selling all the assets, pocketing the money, and then building another type of business never occurred to me. I just did not understand.

Oh, if only I could go back to that point now, with my current knowledge! But of course, that is not possible. Besides, by then it was about more than just money. My own personal identity and self-worth were tied to my business, at least in my own head. *If I let go, would I go on?* I struggled mightily with the thought.

October 2005

My friend Nancy and I partnered together on a property that another realtor owned. He had to move quickly and did not have time to sell the property, so we agreed to pay him on his equity and take over his mortgage payments. We marketed the property and ended up with a real winner for tenants this time.

On paper, the couple looked fine, but talk about dealing with a drama queen! You could have sold tickets to the woman's "winning" or "whining" performances—depending on which end of the phone you were on. Anyway, after being in the house for only a few months, they were already a huge pain. So when they asked if they could purchase the house before the end of the lease, Nancy and I readily agreed.

At the couple's request, I provided the name of one of my lenders so they could obtain financing. Now keep in mind that I actually talk to the people that I do business with, so why the couple thought I would not talk to this lender is beyond me. Anyway, a week later, I received a call from my lender. She had just met with the couple and had them fill out a loan application. They listed on the form that they had ten thousand dollars for a down payment. The lender asked the source of the down payment, since that must be documented, and the couple informed her that they were planning on suing their landlord and that this was what they were estimating the settlement to be.

What do you know, but twenty-four hours later, I was notified that a bi-fold door had just fallen and hit the woman on the head. The story only grew more bizarre from there. After forty-five days of numerous calls to attorneys, insurance agents, hospitals, and my real estate broker, Nancy and I ended up paying them about a thousand dollars to sign a waiver and move. Once again I asked myself if this landlord thing was really working out.

December 2005

A friend of mine found a house priced at what seemed like a below-market price. We decided to purchase the house, fix it up, and then sell it. By this time, I had already done a couple of "fix and flips," but always on lower-end homes. This house cost $436,000, with a monthly mortgage payment of four thousand dollars. Nevertheless, we moved ahead with our plans and purchased the house in December 2005. The rehab was completed by February 2006, and we put it back on the market, anticipating a profit of ninety thousand dollars.

By the end of 2005, I had a net worth of more than five million dollars, with fourteen properties and three parcels of land. I was exhausted, to be sure, but the thrill of the hunt and the adrenaline rush made it all worthwhile. I closed forty-two real estate transactions that year, not including my own. God, of course, was still a real part of my life, but my time with Him was greatly limited. I was not depending on Him as much as I had a couple of years ago. I once again began to think that I was in control.

7

Year 2006: The Wind Picks Up

The market started to slow down. My realtor business in particular was quite a bit slower, so now I had to spend much more time helping my clients find new tenants for their properties. Because of the glut of rental properties on the market, finding and keeping tenants for my clients became a full-time job—one, I might add, in which I was paid very little. Between my own fourteen tenants and the other twenty-five properties of my investors, I began to tire of the issues involved with landlording. This was not going according to all the real-estate guru books.

Considering the payments on the land, the fix-and-flip home, and all of my mortgages, my monthly cash outlay was eight thousand dollars more than what I brought in with rents. Oftentimes the amount was even higher if a tenant failed to pay their rent or I had a vacancy. On top of this, I still had my own personal bills to pay. Combined it was a huge amount to cover each month.

My business partner on the fix-and-flip house soon became unable to pay her share of the mortgage. So that I meant I faced an additional two thousand dollars to pay out every month. My commissions were no longer sufficient to feed the monster I had created. In order to pay the mounting bills, I was forced to refinance several of the rental properties and pull out some of the equity. A short term solution at best, as now the rent amount did not cover the increased mortgage payment. And the monster grew.

The snowball began to roll downhill and quickly gained both speed and size. *What should I do? What direction should I turn? Maybe if I just hold on, this will pass quickly and I will get through it.* The worried thoughts somersaulted through my mind. Night after night, I would awaken around 2:00 a.m., wondering what to do next, how to pay the bills, what I could change? The stress took its toll on me. My fear of failure was very real, almost palpable at times.

February 2006

As we were just getting started in a meeting one day, I calmly took a sip of coffee. But suddenly I could not breathe! I actually spit the coffee onto the poor guy sitting across the table from me. I was not choking; I just could not breathe. I could not inhale, and I could not exhale. All I could do was to gasp desperately for air. The lady next to me hit me on the back, and I started to cough. Finally, I was able to take a breath. Completely puzzled, I had absolutely no idea what the problem might be.

May 2006

I had another episode in which I just stopped breathing. I promised my husband that the next time it happened, I would go to the doctor.

July 2006

My husband was now more than tired of helping me get houses ready to rent. So I convinced my brother Troy that it would be an easy way for him to make some extra money on a Saturday. He agreed, and we made plans to work at my latest abandoned house.

On the appointed day, we met at the site, only to be faced with a house left in worse condition than any other property I have ever owned. This house, which had been occupied by a single man with two small kids, had passed *filthy* nine months ago.

I truly do not think the bathtub had ever been cleaned in the eighteen months the tenant lived there. I used every cleaning product imaginable in an effort to clean that tub. It literally took me two hours to get it somewhat presentable. Then I was faced with the daunting task of cleaning the rest of the house, which was equally as bad. Anyway, poor Troy said he would bag all junk and trash and haul it out to the driveway, where we had made arrangements for a special trash pickup. Needless to say, it took him many hours just to see the floor in that house.

Several hours into his project, he laughingly brought into the house three mannequin heads that he had found in the garage. We had no idea where the bodies were or why the guy had them, but they were a great source of entertainment for us. Then a little while later, Troy brought in something even more surprising: two gallon-sized jars filled with urine! What was that about? Even if the guy was using it for drug testing, did he need two gallons? Is there a huge black market for urine? It was more than disgusting, and with that discovery, Troy said the garage was cleaned out enough. I think he was afraid of what else he might find in there.

After finishing at the house, we both had to go home and take very hot showers before we could go out to dinner. The whole experience was downright creepy. Troy's pay and the very nice dinner at my expense must not have been enough, as he never again volunteered to help me clean out another rental property. I cannot imagine why.

October 2006

Nancy and I started taking some real estate investing classes, hoping to learn some new techniques or glean some different ideas. For nine months, we had to travel to attend the monthly meetings. But we were learning a lot and thought we could implement some new strategies and start generating some income.

During one of those classes, I again stopped breathing. We were in a very large hotel conference room, and I tried to make it out; but before I could get completely out the door, I passed out. I came to very quickly as I started to breathe again.

When I opened my eyes, Nancy was staring down at me, obviously concerned and trying to help. Since we shared a hotel room in order to make our trips more economical, she kindly checked on me several times throughout the night. I do not think she slept at all that night. God again provided a caring friend for me during a scary situation. This was another huge blessing raining down on me.

The next day, I again stopped breathing. I knew there was no getting out of going to the doctor this time. Several weeks later and after many tests, the doctors decided that now, at forty-two years of age, I had asthma. I had never had a breathing problem in my entire life; but now, at least once if not more every day, I would stop breathing. It was a little scary. I felt for the kids who live with asthma every day of their lives, but at the same time, I couldn't help thinking that the stress of my financial burdens had much more to do with my episodes than did asthma.

December 2006

One Sunday in December, I sat in my car in the huge parking lot at church. I was so exhausted from the stress of everything and from the strange breathing episodes that I did not think I had enough energy to walk from my car into the church. I decided to stay where I was and read my Bible, knowing God would understand.

In my devotional readings, I was finishing up the book of Job. Several things dawned on me as I sat in my car reading that morning. Job went through a lot. He lost everything: his children, his wealth, his livestock, and his health. But that morning I realized that Job's struggles did not last just a couple of days or a month. No, they probably lasted several months, maybe even years. He and his friends did not have a couple of conversations over a glass of camel's milk and then God appeared to them and spoke. No, this was probably a long, drawn-out process.

Job probably had good days and then some not-so-great days. He might have had times of doubt and days filled with grief, and maybe he even feared for his life. He couldn't help wondering why it had all happened; his heart was filled with many unanswered questions. As he endured his extended period of time in the wilderness, I'm sure he started to wonder if he would ever get out, just like we do when we face our trials.

Pondering the words, I read the study notes from the last chapter. It read: "Job repented of his attitude and acknowledged God's great power and perfect justice. We sin when we angrily ask, 'If God is in control, how could He let this happen?' Because we are locked into time, unable to see beyond today, we cannot know the reasons for everything that happens. Will you trust God with your unanswered questions? Are you using what you cannot understand as an excuse for your lack of trust? Admit to God that you don't even have enough faith to trust Him. True faith begins in such humility." [5]

Wow! This really hit me hard. Did I have enough faith to trust God with my unanswered questions? I had an entire list of them, and I asked them every night at 2:00 a.m. while waiting for sleep. I had to admit that I had sinned and did not have enough faith to trust in what I could not understand. I had to acknowledge that my lack of understanding and my questions did not change one thing for the omniscient, all-knowing, and never-changing God who is in charge of the whole universe.

Broken, I humbly cried right there in my car. I asked God for His forgiveness, for not being able to trust Him with my unanswered questions. I began to realize again that everything I had came from Him, including every precious breath. It took my loss of such an unconscious necessity as breathing for me to realize how much I had taken so many other blessings for granted. I began to list my blessings rather than my problems and questions and thanked Him for each one.

That day, sitting in my car in that parking lot, I made a conscious decision to focus on the blessings that God was raining down on me rather than on the problems, heartache, and fear that the world was throwing at me. We each have the ability to make that choice. With my focus now back on God, He provided me with another rain shower: I did not experience another breathing episode from that morning on. Praise to the Lord of mercy!

God provided me with eighteen closed transactions for the year. That was a huge pay cut from the previous year's forty-two commission checks, but all the bills were paid and our daily bread supplied. The Lord's Prayer really starts to mean something to you when you are literally asking for your daily bread.

God continued to show Himself, to provide, and to grant peace whenever the darkness started to creep in. But I had to look for it; I had to ask for it. One of the biggest lessons I learned is that being a Christian does not mean it always works out the way we think it should. It does not mean that all hardships, or burdens are removed. It does not mean problems get solved in mere days or even weeks, but sometimes it takes months, years, or decades.

In the beginning, I often cried out for God to take me out of the wilderness, to make all of my problems just go away. But slowly I learned to change the prayer and instead ask for the strength to make it through the wilderness, knowing that I did not possess the ability to get through it on my own. And by His power, He gave me the strength to do it.

As I relied on His help rather than on my strength and power, I was able to keep going in my wilderness journey. The words of Scripture took on new meaning: "My grace is sufficient for you" (2 Cor. 12:9), and "I can do all things through him who gives me strength" (Phil 4:13). I was beginning to understand that trials are sometimes given to us to force us to our knees or to cause us to fall facedown, where we cry out for Abba Father to help us because there is no possible way to make it through the darkness without Him.

8

Year 2007: Here Comes the Haboob

January 2007

E ven though I had improved physically, I was still struggling financially. The market was now past slow—it had tanked. Consequently, I had very few clients. Property values plummeted, so refinancing in order to stay afloat was no longer an option. I juggled funds, I worried some days, and I prayed often.

During those trying days, whenever I concentrated on God's blessings and what He had done for me in the past, a sense of peace prevailed. But as soon as I started to look at my situation from my viewpoint, panic and fear set in. Once again I struggled to take my eyes off my situation and look solely to God. This was a pattern that I kept repeating, and I wondered if I would ever learn to truly trust completely.

The stress I experienced was very real, and I tried hard not to let it get the best of me. But, the monster kept growing. Not knowing what else to do, I started using my personal funds to pay company bills. I kept reminding myself that God was in control, that He knew what was happening, and that everything would be okay. But so often at 2:00 a.m., I would lie awake in bed, unable to shut down my mind. Gazing at the stars, I was often reminded of the great Creator, and it would help me to relax and fall asleep.

During one of my training courses, I had the thought that I should buy a commercial property, rezone it, and then sell it for a profit. Of course, that had been the topic of our training for the past several months, but this was the first time I had the distinct impression that I should move forward with the idea. All the way home, I prayed about whether this was the right course of action for me to take. When I arrived home, I talked to my husband, who was more interested in a commercial adventure than he was in a residential one. With his support, I found a five-acre parcel that was part of an eighty-acre cornfield located right on the corner of two major freeways. Nancy agreed to partner with me.

The lot was listed for $1.36 million dollars. Wow! That was a lot of cash, and there was no way I could buy the lot. I told my family that I was going to try and raise $1.4 million and that I felt this project was for God's glory. My prayer was not just for money, as I know God is not a genie in a bottle, but I truly wanted Him to make Himself known to both me and my family. I knew it was impossible for me to raise the money, rezone the lot, and then sell it. I knew there was absolutely no way I could do any of it. But I did relish the opportunity to trust God in something so visual that the outcome could not be denied. I asked my parents to pray with me during the next thirty days, specifically that God's name would somehow be glorified through this project.

Then I started talking to people and put together a packet about the lot, the location, and the potential. I talked to everyone I could think of, looking for investors to financially support the project. I had thirty days to raise the money and prayed that if God wanted me to move forward, He would provide the financing.

I eventually found an investor who was interested in the project; he committed to putting up the entire $1.4 million. We moved forward with our due diligence, and Nancy and I each put up ten thousand dollars as earnest money. I borrowed the money from my home-equity line of credit, my only source of funds at this point.

Two days away from having the earnest money become nonrefundable, I could not reach the investor to confirm details. Nancy and I were at another real estate class, and I was frantically trying to figure out what to do. I finally reached the investor and was informed that the project he was working on had been delayed. He did not have the money to go forward.

But I am not one to give up easily. At the airport, waiting to go home, I talked to a few people from our group, and someone suggested that I ask for an extension from the seller. As soon as I arrived home, I drafted an extension letter. Thankfully, I received an extension on both the closing and the period before our earnest money became nonrefundable. I then had another thirty days to raise the $1.4 million.

But now the question was whom I should talk to next. I had already exhausted my very skinny Rolodex, so I decided to ask the sellers one more time if they would be interested in carrying the note. Then I got the idea to sweeten the deal for their realtor and offered him twenty-five hundred dollars of my commission if they agreed to it. Several days later, I received their answer: it was a no. Four elderly gentlemen owned the land, and three of the four were okay with my proposal, but the fourth one was not. However, the agent asked if he could still have the bonus if he found someone else to do the deal. I agreed.

I was still talking to anyone who might be interested in our project, even those who had already said no. A couple of weeks went by, and then the realtor called and said he had an investor who might be interested in the project. He had just sold the bank he owned and wanted to do something like this. We made arrangements to speak to him in a couple of days.

Again Nancy and I were out of town, but we found a quiet place to make our call. I was very nervous. I knew that I really did not have many answers, and I knew I did not have the experience to pull this deal off. Furthermore, I was intimidated by the fact that the prospective investor was a former bank president and owner. Nevertheless, we placed the call and spoke with the man. I hoped my voice was not really as shaky as it sounded to me. I was not sure how much confidence I was projecting, but I was doing my best.

Before calling, I had asked God for His favor and to give me the words to say, and what do you know? The guy was interested and wanted to see the land at the end of the week. After seeing it, he committed to one million dollars and said that we needed to bring the remaining four hundred thousand dollars to the table to make the deal work. With that amount, we could close on the land and replace the earnest money that Nancy and I had already put into the deal. So I got back on the phone.

At the beginning of this project, one of the first persons that I had called was a friend of mine from California who was experienced in commercial projects. I decided to call him again and let him know that I had a million dollars and just needed four hundred thousand more dollars. Within a few days, actually only thirty minutes before our earnest money was to be released to the seller, my friend called to say that he and another friend would put up the four hundred thousand dollars. Praise God! In sixty days, He raised $1.4 million, not just once, but twice. What a visual testimony to His involvement in our lives! I was both thrilled and scared to death.

We had one year to get the lot rezoned and sold, neither of which I had any clue on how to proceed. Fortunately, my deadline was predicated on the due date of my balloon payment on the financing so I did not have to make any mortgage payments during that time. I moved ahead, trusting God.

The project gave me something positive to work on, but my financial burden was still very real. I could hide in the closet, but the monster was still lurking outside. I was still waking at 2:00 a.m., still questioning, still praying, and still crying out for answers. God had just performed a miracle, but still I could not relax. The situation seemed overwhelming. I was running out of money, options, and time.

October 9, 2007

One evening in October, I was attending a women's Bible study. It had been a very long, hard day. I had spent the day in tears, panic attacks, and prayer. Basically, I was a complete wreck. Barb, the study leader, taught the lesson and then sang an old hymn that I love. The timeless words touched my soul in a way that only God can do:

Through It All [6]

I've had many tears and sorrows,
I've had questions for tomorrow,
There've been times I didn't know right from wrong.
But in every situation,
God gave blessed consolation,
That my trials come only to make me strong.

Through it all,
Through it all,
I've learned to trust in Jesus,
I've learned to trust in God.

Through it all,
Through it all,
I've learned to depend upon His Word.

I thank God for the mountains,
And I thank Him for the valleys,
I thank Him for the storms He brought me through.
For if I'd never had a problem,
I wouldn't know that He could solve them,
I'd never know what faith in God could do.

I cried the entire time Barb was singing the song. I was sure everyone must be looking at me; I could see Barb herself wondering what was going on. But my life had been shattered. To me, the song was a sign from God that He was still there and still cared, even though I didn't understand what was happening in my life and could not fix my problems.

We broke into our small groups, and I asked a question: "Where is the line between being persistent and being stupid?" I had tried to hold everything together for so long, thinking if I could just hang in there a little bit longer, everything would get better. But is there a point at which being persistent becomes stupid? I think I took the group aback with my question. The group leader, Robin, prayed for the Holy Spirit's guidance and then proceeded to try to answer my question. I am afraid the rest of the group did not get to ask any questions that night.

As a group, we decided that maybe I had crossed the line between persistence and stupidity, as my life was so out of balance. If I sold the properties, which I saw as giving up a ministry, perhaps God would lead me to something else. This conversation began an awesome and blessed friendship with Robin and another woman in the group, Tammy. I went home feeling a little bit better.

A couple of days later, I sent an e-mail to Robin and Barb to express my appreciation for their love and ministry:

From: Jami
To: Robin and Barb
Subject: Thank you
Date: Thursday, October 11, 2007

Barb and Robin,

I want to thank you both for being an answer to prayer on Tuesday night. Both of you touched my life with the hand of God that I so desperately needed. My business has been failing over the last two years, and I have been very persistent to make it work, even if I had to hold it together with duct tape. I have been praying that God would lead and guide me and grant me peace. It has been an emotional roller-coaster ride.

In December 2006, when things were very bad, I surrendered myself to God. He did grant me peace, and it looked like things might be turning around. However, as the new year wore on, I became increasingly weary.

Tuesday was the day the proverbial camel's back was broken. I spent most of the day in prayer, panic attacks, and tears. I needed to know that it was okay to let go of this job that I really did see as a ministry. I needed to know that letting go did not equal a failure in God's eyes; I needed to know that He still has a plan for me, as stated in Jeremiah 29:11, one of my personal promise verses.

Barb, your lesson, and especially the song you sang at the end, had me in tears. I knew that God was saying, "I know, I care, I love you." I actually sing that song quite often during my quiet time. Okay, not nearly as well as you did, but the words are powerful to me. With only about ten people in the class, how could you possibly pick an old-time hymn that was going to minister to someone so effectively? It was only by the grace of God.

Robin, I heard much more than the words you spoke later in the evening. I found it interesting that you asked God for the words to say right before you spoke to me, because He certainly answered that prayer. But God was not done just because we had our closing prayer; He still had two more things to say to me. As we were walking to our cars, you said that you were an ex-pastor, which I took as God telling me that your words were coming from Him and to trust them. Then you shared that you had quit your church ministry to move to Phoenix. That was just what I needed to know: that God may give you a ministry, and at times it comes to an end, but He will use you in a new ministry. I knew this in my head, but I needed that confirmation in my heart on Tuesday night.

I prayed all the way home and told God that I felt I needed to end my business and that I would trust Him (1) to figure out how to sell fourteen rental properties and three parcels of land in a down market and (2) to lead me to the next thing that I am to be involved in. Tuesday night was the first night I slept soundly in over fifteen days. On Wednesday, while my husband and I were working on a rental house to get it ready to rent again, I told him of my decision. He was relieved, happy—I'm not sure exactly what, but I did get a kiss out of the deal. :) Maybe he was just tired of painting.

So I want to thank you again and let you know that the time and energy that you both spend to make Tuesday nights happen is worth it. God is using you in a very real way.

Have a wonderful day and a great weekend.

Jami

Robin, Tammy, and I soon discovered that we shared quite a few common interests, and our friendship grew. As the women's Bible study drew to an end, the three of us decided to continue to meet for prayer and Bible study. Never before had I had such strong Christian women friends in my life. Their friendship was truly a godsend, equivalent to a whole springtime of rain showers. To this day, I cannot thank God enough for these women.

My family, of course, was wonderful, but this friendship was something different. Sometimes we just met for a cup of coffee, but we would still pray. I honestly am not sure if I could have made it without their friendship; I know for a fact that without their prayers, I would not have.

November 2007

The more Robin, Tammy, and I met, the more impacted I was by Robin's prayers. They were so different from any other prayers I had ever heard or experienced. There was a power, a boldness, about them. I felt so comforted whenever she prayed for me.

I could keenly sense the presence of God, and I was drawn to it, like a moth to a light.

Curious, I asked Robin how she had learned to pray like that. She responded by encouraging me to study God's Word. I did read my Bible, but my prayers sounded so wimpy compared to hers. I could not explain what was different, but I knew I wanted it—whatever it was. I wanted it for myself, of course, but I also wanted to be able to comfort others when I prayed for them like Robin comforted me.

December 2007

It had taken five months to get the land project started, and it would typically require another six months to get an empty lot rezoned. But what was supposed to take six months, God accomplished in under sixty days. I watched God open doors and miraculously work on my behalf on this project. City planners, neighbors, architects, commercial brokers—everyone and everything just came together with absolutely no hiccups. It was amazing how quickly and smoothly the entire process went. Though grateful, I was aware that I was still in way over my head. Once the lot was rezoned, we still needed to find a hotel or retail developer to purchase it. I started working the phones again, trying to drum up interest.

By the end of the year, I again had eighteen closed transactions, just like the year before. This paid most of my personal bills, but the shortfall from the business made for a huge juggling act. The monster was still alive and well.

But even though things at times seemed over-whelming, I knew deep inside that God was still there. I did not doubt His presence, for He was now a very real part of my everyday life. I spent time every morning reading His Word, and while driving, which I did a lot of, I listened only to praise music on Christian radio. I knew these two things, combined with much prayer, were making a huge difference in my life. More rain spattered gently on my trail.

9

Year 2008: Thunder and Lightning

In early January, six of my tenants called to tell me that they were breaking their leases and moving out. Since beginning this work five years earlier, I had never had six vacancies all at once. The end was inevitable.

With that awareness dawning, I wrote the following e-mail to my family:

January 30, 2008
To: My family

Good morning,

It is the beginning of a new period of my life. As you know, change is somewhat difficult for me. I have been fighting it for several months, but I believe I am to the point of accepting that Next

Step Properties, LLC needs to change and quite possibly go out of business altogether. It is with a heavy heart that I make this statement in such a concrete way. However, it has finally become quite obvious that no matter how many hours I work, how much I worry about things, and how much I hope and wish that things were different, this is the reality of the situation.

I was given a great gift five years ago, and that was the opportunity to try. I was concerned that I really did not see myself as a creative or outside-the-box thinker. In fact, I feared that I might not be able to think at all! But God showed me that I could do all of those things, and as a result, the business was a success.

I went into my business asking God to lead it and be the CEO. He has. I am proud to have been a part of the process, and I know that many lives were touched and changed. However, as manager of the assets God placed before me, I made poor choices. Some were made out of greed, some out of excitement, and some were due to bad information; nevertheless, the choices were mine and mine alone. Therefore, I take full responsibility for those choices and their consequences. I unfortunately and unknowingly have pulled you, my family, into this web; and my choices will have an effect on all of you, but mainly Kim and Jeff and Judi, by which I am deeply saddened.

So here we are: an ending yet a new beginning. I am putting as much effort into closing down the business as I put into building it up. It may take several years before I can completely liquidate all the assets, but the first steps are being taken. It is my continued prayer that God would give me integrity, wisdom, guidance, and peace as I move forward. It is also my prayer that God would find me a worthy manager of His resources again and that I might have a second chance at another business.

I want to assure each of you that it is my deepest desire to save your credit and to pay back every cent you invested with the company. I do still have the assets that secured your investments, and each of you will be paid as soon as the assets are sold. It is my desire not to sell the assets at a fire or wholesale price unless absolutely necessary, thus preserving as much of the equity as possible. This, of course, may lengthen the time it takes to completely liquidate.

At this time, I am not sharing this news with my private investors or anyone outside of my immediate family. They, too, will be paid back, but I do not want to cause them any undue distress, since they are all unaware of the current financial situation.

This morning as I look at my life, I am very blessed. I have a husband who provides me with unconditional love and support. I have a family who also loves and cares for me unconditionally. My health is still good. I have learned so much about so many things, met so many good people, and basically had a lot of fun along the way. I will take those blessings and move forward, not in fear, but in the knowledge that with God anything is possible, knowing that this truly is not the end of anything but a time to regroup, redefine, and gain a fresh start.

With that said, I know the next year may be difficult. However, God will get me through this desert, and I will be stronger for it in the end. Thank you for your continued prayers.

Jami
Manager of Next Step Properties, LLC

February 2008

Even though I made a commitment to close down the business, I had no intention of having the properties, now mostly vacant, go into foreclosure. But what options did I have? I was out of money; I had no reserves; I had spent almost every dime trying to keep all of the properties going. The monster laughed, and I felt like such a failure.

For the first time in my life, hard work, perseverance, money, and prayer did not change the situation. To me, foreclosure represented the ultimate defeat. I had always had perfect credit, and yes, I was proud of it. Foreclosure seemed like letting God down, failing at the task He had given me. I had made a promise to the bank to pay back the money borrowed, so foreclosure would be breaking that promise and letting them down. I felt as though I had let everyone and everything down!

Troubled in heart, I paid a visit to our family pastor, desperate to know that God would forgive me. Of course, in my heart, I knew that He would, but I needed verbal reassurance. Dr. R. spoke with wisdom and kindness, pointing out that many things were outside of my control. I could not control the market, I could not control my tenants moving out, I could not control any of it. He assured me that God does not look at your FICO score before He lets you enter heaven.

Then he said something that really struck me. He said that sometimes you have to exchange currency. His point was that the banks knew the risk of lending money to me or to anyone else, for that matter. As part of the existing mortgage agreement, they were willing to exchange cash for the property. Foreclosure was not letting them down, but instead, it was just another form of payment. But most important of all, he assured me that my net worth did not equal my self-worth.

These last two comments really helped me a lot. Since then I have shared them with many other people facing the same situation, and I hope it encouraged them like it did me. I left the pastor's office knowing that I would not be selling the properties for a profit. Rather, they were headed down the path of foreclosure and short sales.

I was very systematic in the process and started defaulting on the land and the vacant houses. I spoke to my brother about his land, and we agreed that it also needed to either be sold as a short sale or go into foreclosure. As bad as I felt for myself, my guilt was tenfold knowing that I had caused this pain and hardship for my brother and his wife. Real estate was supposed to have helped him and been something positive in his life.

The downward spiral now began. As hard as it was to hold everything together, letting go was even worse.

February 15

For the first time in my life, I did not pay a bill sitting on my desk. Not just one but six mortgages just sat there, unpaid. The collection calls quickly followed. Every time the phone rang, it was an audible reminder of my failure, and it rang endlessly. After the second month, the seemingly never-ceasing calls actually increased. Sometimes they called me three or four times a day per loan.

Failure! Failure! Failure! I tried hard to ignore the thought pounding through my brain. I tried to find solace by telling myself that it was not my fault, but I was not overly successful at it. Only by the grace of God did I make it through each day. I knew He had not left me, but at times He did seem pretty far away. I did have some good days, but others were more difficult to get through.

To add to my problems, not only did I have to deal with the short sales and the collection calls, but I also had to face the fact that I had no clients. That meant I had no income. I began to wonder if all this would ever end. I had seen what depression could do to a person, so I prayed that God would protect my mind from all the negative things around me and keep me from succumbing to depression.

March 2008

By March I was struggling to make decisions and second guessing the ones that I did make. Since all my previous decisions had proven bad, I was now afraid of making another wrong choice. Even the simplest decisions required extra time for me to process.

April 2008

April brought new challenges and ushered in change for my family. Here is part of an e-mail I sent to Robin and Tammy on April 8 that expressed my sentiments:

Robin and Tammy,

I wanted to share an answer to prayer, even though my heart is somewhat heavy. As you know, my grandmother has been in chronic pain for my entire life. She has endured much yet possessed a love of life like I have never seen. She passed away this morning. The prayer of my family had been that God would be merciful and gracious to both her and my mom when the time came. This prayer was answered in a truly remarkable way.

I went up to Prescott yesterday to visit, and Gram was in and out of it. She recognized that I had changed my hairstyle and told me that she did not like it; then she fell back asleep. :) Later she wanted to sit up, so I helped her to a more elevated position, but she tired before getting all the way up and lay back down.

Anyway, while I was there, the hospice nurse came by. She told us that Gram probably had a couple of more weeks to a month, as her vitals were strong and she still had quite a bit of strength. During the course of this conversation, we got a phone call from Colorado that Gram's sister Jean was failing and had only twenty-four to seventy-two hours to live. We did not tell this news to Gram. There were six sisters in Gram's family, with Grandma and Jean being the two oldest and the closest. They were only nine months apart in age.

At 10:00 p.m. yesterday, Mom got the call that Jean had received the Lord at 4:00 p.m. (an answered prayer, as my mother has prayed for her unsaved family for many years), was baptized, and passed away at 9:00 p.m. Shortly before moving to Arizona, my grandmother accepted Christ as her Savior, so both sisters are now in heaven. Praise God!

Mom went in to tell Gram the news, but Gram was so happy, laughing and talking to someone whom only she could see, that Mom decided to tell her the news in the morning. At 6:15 this morning, my mom went in to check on Gram. She had somehow, with a fused back, a fused knee, a torn rotator cuff, and several other ailments, managed to climb over the bed rails and was lying on the floor. Her face was still warm, but she was gone. She died nine hours after her sister.

My mother never heard anything on the baby monitor, though she normally could hear even Gram's breathing. It must have been peaceful; Grandma did not cry out, nor was she afraid. What an answer to our prayers!

We all went up to Prescott again today to help, and my cousin reminded us that the third sister had passed away on April 8, 2007. So all three of the sisters who have passed away died on the same day, which is only ten days from the anniversary of my grandfather's death.

It was a peaceful day. We all know that my grandmother is finally out of pain. She is in heaven with Jesus and with my grandfather. I am sure they are dancing tonight, which was their favorite pastime. My grandfather was deaf, but he can hear the music now. My grandmother had a fused and short leg, but she can once again wear a long gown and high heels, a dream of hers. And to make the party even more special, they have two of the sisters and their spouses to celebrate with them. I can see it now.

I will be heading to Colorado on Thursday, and the services will be on Tuesday. I should be back in Arizona the following Thursday. An important chapter of my life is now complete. All four of my grandparents were very special to me and had a huge impact on my life, Gram especially. I am blessed to have had them in my life for so long. I have no regrets. I visited Grandma often, I took flowers, she knew she was loved, and I knew she loved me. God is merciful and gracious.

My folks are doing okay. After the service, Mom and Dad are going to take a week or so in coming back home to just spend time together. It will be good for them both. My grandmother has lived with them for eleven years, so it will be different when they return, but they will be fine.

God provided many gentle showers to my family during this week. His grace and mercy were so very obvious. A week or so later, I went to my mom's house to help her clean out Grandma's stuff. She had downsized considerably when she sold her house in Colorado and moved in with my parents in Prescott, so she really did not have more than what could fit in her bedroom. We put everything in piles: stuff to go to the Goodwill store, stuff to throw out, stuff to keep, and stuff to give to the museum. Then we bagged the piles. When we were done, three trash bags of stuff were left for us to deal with.

As I sat there on the floor, it really hit me that life boils down to this. As much as I wanted to make Gram's "treasures" important to me, they were not. After an entire lifetime, her earthly possessions really were nothing more than stuff in a bag. I realized nothing really matters other than what we invest into others. The memories, the lessons taught, the laughter—those last long after we are gone, but not our stuff. I decided right then to try harder to invest more into more people, as that is the only way my life is going to count for anything.

That day will stick with me for the remainder of my life.

May 2008

Prior to my own personal financial meltdown, I had dealt with a lot of people who were facing financial or credit challenges. The largest majority of my tenants fit into this category. Through the years, I had assisted many people with setting up budgets and trying to better manage their finances. I did feel for them and wanted to help them, but I had a hard time understanding why it seemed that they did not care more. My advice to them was always the same. I encouraged them to get out of debt, spend less than they made, cut up their credit cards, not to use payday loans, open their mail, and take care of bills as they came in—all the things that work when you have money.

Now as the collection calls continued and I had no money for the payments, I began to feel helpless, defeated, and discouraged. It seemed there was no way back, no light at the end of this dark financial tunnel. For the first time in my life, I now understood the other side of the equation for those with financial difficulties. I understood, for example, why the mail is not opened. If there is no money to pay the bills anyway, why bother opening them? I understood that feeling of defeat, because no matter how hard I tried, I was always faced with another bill, another collection call, and another reminder of my shortcomings. I understood feeling like, *This is never going to end, so why not spend what little I have on something pleasurable?* I understood why so many of my tenants had not made more of an effort to help themselves even after I offered to help them. Never before had it worked out, so why bother to expend the energy in an attempt to make it better this time?

We live in a world of hopelessness, but I had never before truly recognized its extent. After going through my own financial crisis, I apologized to several people and asked for their forgiveness, admitting that I had not truly understood what they were going through and how hopeless they had felt. If nothing else good ever came out of my situation, at least I could now truly say I understood that feeling of hopelessness. I now had true empathy for those facing credit and financial challenges.

As the year went on, I realized again how very important the message I had been given at the beginning of 2008 was: "Your self-worth does not equal your net worth." I wanted to get that message out and encourage others with it. My path began crossing that of many good, responsible people who, like me, were facing challenges they had never experienced before. I prayed that they, too, would realize that they amount to more than their bank account balance or FICO number. *One setback does not define a life.*

Here is another e-mail I sent to Robin and Tammy as the month drew near to its close. I was excited with the prospect of what might be unfolding.

May 23, 2008
To: Robin and Tammy
Re: Answer to prayer?

Okay, we need more prayer time together! We prayed on Wednesday night, and on Thursday I received a call from my commercial broker that he was taking a hotel developer to look at the land on Sunday.

Then I got a call from the city's economic developer, who was following up on an e-mail that I had sent to him earlier in the week. Four of the city guys were at the International Shopping Center Expo in Vegas this week looking for developers, tenants, etc., for the eighty acres that my five-acre parcel is part of. During the expo, Paul from the city group talked to a hotel chain that is very interested in building in the area. We are only in the very early stages, as this has all transpired in the last twenty-four hours, but it looks like we might sell two acres to the hotel, which would net me $800,000, and I would retain the other three acres.

God would then only have to point me to the guy
with $300,000 to pay off my balloon payment of
$1.1 million by July 12.

This may not work out, and God may have other
plans, but it is exciting to watch it unfold. If only
I could let God handle all of my life like I have
let Him handle this project, my hair would still be
naturally blonde!

Jami

The deal did not unfold as I had hoped; the hotel
bought on the other side of the freeway.

June 2008

Since the commercial lot had not yet sold, I asked
for extensions on the balloon payment from the three
investors holding the notes. The investor who gave us
a million dollars did not want to extend the note, but
the other two investors agreed to an extension for an
additional year. So I once again needed to raise $1.1
million in order to pay off the first mortgage by July
12.

But I had nowhere to turn. I had no contacts,
and really, I had nothing to offer anyone to make the
project enticing. Someday it would be a great lot in a
good location with access, but right now no one was
looking for retail or hotel space. In fact, Phoenix had
been blacklisted for new retail-development money.

I started a thirty-day prayer vigil to bring my
request before God, asking for His blessing and asking
that His will be done, as this project had always been
about making Him known. At this time in my life, I did

not really know much about fasting, but I decided to abstain from all beverages with the exception of water for thirty days—no diet Coke, no coffee, not even milk on my cereal. Every time I wanted something to drink, I would pray about the lot. In short order, however, I discovered that I was actually worrying about the lot and begging God to intervene rather than stepping out in faith. So I changed the fasting rules to every time I desired a drink, I would name five blessings or quote a Scripture promise verse. Yes, I played mind games with myself all the time, and sometimes they actually worked! As I focused on God instead of the request, peace would overtake me.

I continued going to the prayer hill at church every Friday morning at daybreak for an extended time in prayer. I also continued to receive my daily Bible verse from the radio station KLOVE, and on June 14, 2008, it was especially meaningful: "For I am the Lord, your God, who takes hold of your right hand and says to you, Do not fear; I will help you" (Isa. 41:13). This gave me peace about the commercial lot, but even more so with my other financial stresses. Whenever I started to panic, I would actually hold my right hand with my left hand and quote the verse. I knew God was there!

June 20

As I was heading out the door to an appointment that morning, I felt hungry, even though I had eaten breakfast. I walked over to the refrigerator to grab something, but my legs gave out. My husband helped me to the couch, and both of my legs and then my arms began to jump almost convulsively. I had not lost consciousness, so it was not a seizure. I wondered what was going on.

July 2008

On July 2, I received notification that several of our credit cards had been canceled or the available limits dropped and/or interest rates raised. Though I figured this was coming, it was still hard to swallow. God was most definitely working on my pride, as these were very humbling circumstances.

July 10

Things were not getting any easier, and I was very discouraged. I couldn't help but wonder if there might be an easier way. I was not contemplating anything specific, but very dark thoughts were running through my head. However, I kept them to myself.

That day I received a phone call from Tammy, suggesting we go out to dinner for my birthday. Ten minutes later, Robin called, and she also said we should go out to dinner. I reluctantly agreed to their plan, though I did not really feel like celebrating anything.

After we enjoyed a nice dinner together, Robin suggested that we go back to Tammy's house and pray. We did. I opened up and shared with them my dark thoughts and asked for their prayers. Never ask a prayer warrior to pray for you if you do not mean it! The two women laid hands on me and earnestly interceded for me. The Spirit of God was definitely in the room, and He heard our prayers. The dark thoughts were removed and replaced with His peace.

Forty-five minutes later, I was covered in tears and sweat, but it was the good kind, as though I were covered in heavenly raindrops. God is such an awesome, wonderful God, so full of mercy and love. I couldn't help but wonder, *Why do I keep doubting? Has He not proved Himself faithful? Why do I keep letting doubt and fear control my life?*

July 11

We found a source of funding for the five-acre commercial lot; however, they had only half of the required million. We still needed the other half within the next twenty-four hours.

July 12

The next day, we received a tentative commitment for the remaining half million, but I needed some time to pull it all together. The one-million-dollar investor gave us a ten-day extension.

July 16

As suddenly as it all came together, it all fell apart. All the committed funding for the commercial project was canceled. We had it, and then it was gone—just that quickly. The same thing had happened the previous year as well. Was I trapped in the *Groundhog Day* movie or what? It seemed I kept reliving parts of this very long nightmare.

July 18

I decided to go to the prayer hill at church. It was always so peaceful there in the morning—nothing but the birds and insects to distract a person. But I was not in turmoil that day. Remembering the prayer session at Tammy's, I was, in fact, encouraged, despite the events of the week. I pulled out a notebook and started to think about all the lessons I had learned in the past few years.

Here are some of my thoughts from the prayer hill as I dealt with the unwinding of Next Step Properties, LLC and the possible foreclosure on the commercial lot:

- Relationships can and do last even through tough times.
- I am not exempt from trouble, even when I am in God's will.
- I am learning to trust that God is still there holding my hand at all times.
- A strong witness *requires* adversity.
- How I deal with adversity is more important than my getting out of adversity.
- Satan will use worry, fear, busyness, and the feeling of being overwhelmed against me.
- Every possession can be lost.
- Do not focus on the problem; do not let it be the center of every thought and conversation.
- FICO score and net worth do not equal self-worth.
- Business failure does not equal a lack of personal integrity.
- You always have more than someone else and more than you realize.

- Being rich and being poor, both are blessings and curses.
- The meaning of *poor* is different for everyone and can change. Someone can have a thousand dollars in the bank and feel just as poor as someone else does with ten.
- Everyone needs hope; share yours, even if you have only a small amount.
- Rest, but do not stop trusting.
- This season will pass. Get through it; do not avoid it.
- Even the desert has beauty, but it is harder to see at times.
- Godly women are patient and self-controlled, not erratically emotional.
- Anger and frustration only make the problem worse.
- Sometimes you have to step back and just wash the dishes.
- Neither you nor anyone else knows the depth of their faith until it is fully tested.
- Everyone has a different degree of testing as God sees fit. There is no standard test.
- Nothing, nothing can be taken for granted; all is at risk: relationships, money, security, and even the breath in our lungs.
- Not all people are honest; there are wolves. It is okay not to deal with them.
- Being taken advantage of does not equal the Christian walk.
- You cannot be a wise steward and blindly help everyone.

- Sometimes things are out of your control; it does not mean that your integrity is at stake.
- Sometimes you have to change the currency you use.
- Sometimes you want something for someone more than they do.
- Ministry is not easy—actually, it is very hard.
- Life is like the Painted Desert. It is not what you expect, but it is still good and beautiful, if you stop crying long enough to look at it.

I am sure these lessons do not apply to everyone, but it is always good to take time to reflect on the lessons learned through any difficult situation, even if for no other reason than to acknowledge your time in the wilderness. God does not waste a hurt or a tear, but we have to look for the answers in that still, small voice. Sometimes the jewels of life are hidden.

After spending time in prayer and really reflecting on everything, my heart and spirit were further lifted. I felt like rejoicing. Though my circumstances had not changed, my attitude and my renewed dependence on God had indeed changed. I was now emotionally and mentally okay with knowing that the commercial lot would probably go back to the lender. I was at peace and once again surrendered everything to God. Surrender, I know, is a daily act of worship, but I usually didn't do it until things were so out of control that I had no choice. When would I ever learn?

Later that day, I sent an e-mail to my precious family and friends who had stood with me. Here is how I chronicled my thoughts:

July 18, 2008
To: Robin, Tammy, Mom, and Dad (my prayer warriors)

Come, bring the fatted calf and rejoice with me!

From the very beginning, I have always felt and said that I was supposed to be involved with the five-acre commercial lot so that God could show His glory and His might. I also felt that it was not about the real estate, although at times I forgot that part. I was correct on both accounts.

God first showed His power by opening all the doors and leading me to the right people so that the first $1.4 million could be raised for the purchase of the lot. It was impossible for me to raise that much money in thirty days without a miracle from God. When the loan commitment was broken, God proceeded to do another miracle and provided another $1.4 million in the following thirty days. I feel this was to solidify in my mind who truly was the owner of this lot.

Once the lot was purchased, God opened all the doors to allow the rezoning to take place. This was a process in which I had absolutely no experience. But the rezoning took only sixty days instead of the six months that the city told me it would take, and I did not even open my mouth during any of the meetings.

The time came to sell the land, and bolstered by additional prayer warriors, I set off to seek God's favor again. I was in need of $1.1 million and had thirty days to raise the capital. God again was faithful and provided $1.2 million to pay off the balloon payment. But again the loan commitment was broken, and a ten-day extension was granted. Since God had provided on three separate occasions, I was pretty convinced that He would provide again.

As I sat on the prayer hill at church this morning, a new sense of peace and understanding swept over me. I began to write down lessons learned in the past months, and this letter was rolling around in my head as if someone were reading it to me. I realize that God's glory has been shown, that He did do a mighty thing! God has made Himself very visible, but it was not just about the real estate.

In the past thirty days, God has shown me His faithfulness through Kim. Though facing increased financial hardship, my husband has reconfirmed his love for me. His faithfulness during the storm when so many others would have turned and fled is a testimony of his love and is a blessing from God. Instead of running, he has tied our bond of love more tightly.

God also showed me His love and peace through my parents. They always are a rock of love and support. No matter what I am facing, they are there to cheer me on. During this time, they have joined me in prayer and fasting. There were times when my dad would call just to say, "I am praying for you; God is in control." My mom would take my calls and listen to my heart as I cried out my fears for everything that was going on in my life.

God also showed me His grace by providing me with great friends. At no time in my life have I been blessed with such strong friends, where prayer is the center of our visits. At times I felt like Moses, as though Robin and Tammy were holding my arms up, like Joshua and Aaron did for Moses during the battle. When the spiritual battle was at its peak, they stepped up and imparted God's human touch. Their hugs, laughter, and heartfelt prayers were nothing short of a miracle. I wonder if some of their personal battles right now are an attack from the enemy as a result of their taking my battle to the throne of God.

Yes, God has shown Himself to me in a mighty way, and I am grateful. But I wonder if this is everything? Is there more to this story? At this moment, I do not know what will happen in the coming days. It is very likely that the land will go into foreclosure on Wednesday, July 23. But there is a sense of peace, as I know in my heart that the lot was God's and I did everything I could to sell it. He could have provided as He did in the past, but He didn't, so this must be His plan.

As I looked for the reason, a thought was given to me. It took this level of intensity in my life to draw me near the Father's heart in such a completely surrendered manner. I never laid claim to the commercial lot and always knew it belonged to God. Perhaps He provided a very real-world example, one that even I could not miss. Perhaps it took me watching God letting go and allowing this lot to go into foreclosure for me to realize that I, too, can let the rental properties go back to the bank and know I have not failed Him. I need to continue to let go of the fear, the properties, and the illusion of security.

As I continue my wilderness walk and unwind my business and the financial implications surrounding it, I know that God will continue to be there. He will continue to love me and provide for my family. He is faithful. There are many uncertain days ahead for all of us, but God is real and He cares. May my witness be strong as I move forward from this place.

"For I am the Lord, your God, who takes hold of your right hand and says to you, Do not fear; I will help you" (Isa. 41:13).

To His name be the glory,
Jami

July 20

Remarkably, we found another funding source for the commercial lot; however, it required monthly payments of eleven thousand dollars, which I did not have. My friend from California who had paid the four hundred thousand dollars and was in a second-lien position (meaning he would get none of his money back if we could not pay off the gentleman who had put up the one million dollars) finally made the very painful decision that we had to let the property go back to the million-dollar investor in a foreclosure action. This hurt me almost as much as my guilt over my brother's land investment. This action caused my friend to lose four hundred thousand dollars, and there was not one thing I could do about it.

July 23

It was so strange; I kept hearing music at night, like a radio playing in my head. Most of the songs were Christian songs from the radio, but sometimes they were old hymns. Regardless, it made it quite difficult to fall asleep and to stay asleep. I sometimes awoke in the night in the middle of a song. Although I often admonished myself to be quiet, I was not the one singing. It was so weird.

August 2008

I was still struggling to pay the bills. Thus far, I had completed only ten transactions, and there was no new business in the foreseeable future. Kim and I had tapped our life insurance a few months earlier, and our credit cards were pretty well maxed out. There really were no options at this point.

I struggled not to get stressed and fearful—again. The cycle was starting. Every time I started to worry about finances, I would get stressed and scared. Then after a while, I would turn it over to God and receive His peace. I wondered if I would ever stop this roller-coaster ride and simply live a life of faith. But I was not quite there yet.

Right now, the electric bill for our primary residence was sitting on my desk, unpaid for forty-five days. The service was scheduled to be turned off in only a few more days. I asked Kim if we should borrow some money from someone, but he said no. So we waited, and I prayed that God would provide.

A couple of days passed. I decided to go online to check our bank account. I'm not sure why, since I knew it was pretty empty—or at least it was supposed to be. But unbelievably, the available balance was $18,113! *What? There must be a mistake!* I immediately thought. As I looked more closely, I saw a direct deposit from the IRS in the account. Now I knew it was a mistake! I called my accountant, who explained that since I had suffered such a large loss in my business the previous year, he had refiled the taxes from 2005 and gotten this refund.

What? Did we forget to have that conversation when we sat in your office and reviewed the taxes? Did I forget that a check for $18,000 was coming? I silently wondered. I did not really think so; there was simply no human explanation for this. The accountant interrupted my musings and assured me the money was mine to keep. Praise God! Wow, now even the IRS was doing His bidding! I had never in all my life been so excited to pay the electric bill.

The next day my husband brought in the mail. There was a check for nineteen thousand dollars, from the IRS! *What? This must be a duplicate!* I again called the accountant, who explained that out of the refund from the refilled 2005 return, they had taken part of it and applied it towards this year's tax bill. It, too, was being refunded because of our large loss. *Thank God for losses!* I thought. Anyway, we now had thirty-seven thousand dollars to get us through the rest of 2008—just enough. The raindrops of blessings along my path were ever growing.

August 20

On this day, the five acres in no man's land—or better known as Maricopa, Arizona—and the two golf lots in Prescott all went to trustee sale. The purchase of land was a big part of my undoing, so I was glad when these properties were gone and I could forget about them forever.

September 6, 2008

My job allowed me a lot of time by myself in my car as I drove around town. This day I was at peace as I reflected on what had happened over the past couple of years and where I might be going once Next Step Properties, LLC was completely dissolved.

I knew without a doubt that I had been truly blessed. In fact, I could truthfully say I had been blessed by God my entire life. My childhood was good and happy. I had parents who loved me, provided for my needs and wants, and supported me in all things. I had active grandparents for most of my life. My brothers and I were still very close. I canoed in the backcountry of Canada, and I received my pilot's license at the age of fifteen. I received a good education, enjoyed good jobs, saw different parts of the country, and met a lot of great people. I was married to a good man; I had made quite a bit of money; I enjoyed a wonderful home, cars, and clothes; and all of my needs and wants had been met. So without a doubt, I knew I was blessed.

So if I had been blessed for forty years of my life, how could I believe that all of a sudden God was no longer blessing me? If He promised to be with me always and that nothing could ever separate me from His love, how could I assume that He had turned His back on me? If all things work together for good for those who are called, then this, too, could be used by Him for His glory.

The realization dawned in my soul, and I continued to ponder. *I may not understand, but like Job, who am I to ask why? If God knows where the store-*

house of the snow lives, and if He drew the line in the sand and told the ocean that it could not come any closer, then who am I to question Him? So I must still be in His will for me, in spite of my feelings. After all, faith is not an emotion.

Then a new thought crossed my mind: *I know Christ, and I know He only wants good for me, yet during this difficult season, there have been times when I was overcome with fear, panic, and hopelessness. How much more overwhelming must it be for someone who does not know Christ to deal with a financial setback or any other type of wilderness walk!*

That led to an entirely new set of questions rolling through my mind: *How can my situation be used for the good of others? How can I minister to others? How can I take my particular skill set and provide the hope of God to others? Should I write a book, conduct seminars? What? Please God, show me the way I should go. Direct my steps. Are the seeds of a new ministry being planted?*

September 13

I thought I was done with the three parcels of land, but I guess forever only lasts about thirty days. I soon learned the hard way that land is handled differently from residences during the foreclosure process. My learning process began with a guy in a suit handing me legal papers and serving me with a lawsuit for a deficiency of forty-six thousand dollars. When that happens, you know right then that the day is going to be tough!

At this time in the state of Arizona, when a house went into foreclosure or, more accurately, through a trustee sale, the entire amount owed, as long as it was purchase money, was forgiven. You might have to pay taxes on the deficiency (the difference between what was owed and the fair-market value at the time of the trustee sale), but that was it. Not so, however, with raw land.

The first of the deficiency lawsuits was on the five acres in Maricopa. This was just the beginning of the foreclosures and lawsuits, but I was already wondering if all this would ever end. I never imagined it would take so much work and effort to give back these properties. Of course, I had no choice but to work through this, but I was weary from everything.

We called an attorney, but after a month or so, we decided we could not afford to keep him on retainer. That meant we would have to self-represent, an idea that more than overwhelmed me. My husband, however, rose to the challenge and did all sorts of research on the court process. I could never have made it through this without him. And to think, this was the land he had been so adamant that I not buy. I knew how lucky I was to have him stick with me through all this.

All throughout the process, I knew there was a problem with the deficiency amount that the bank was reporting. We had an escrow holdback tied to the account, but I was not getting credit for that. After several months of arguing, I was at my wit's end. I finally turned to God in prayer and asked that He just intervene and make the bank understand. Very shortly the bank's escrow department acknowledged that they were indeed holding forty thousand dollars in the account. After those funds were released, the bank dismissed the suit in January 2009.

As I recall it now, it all sounds so easy, but it was actually very intimidating at the time. As far as I was concerned, I was definitely swimming in uncharted waters. But I had to repeat this experience two more times: once with my golf-course lot and then with my brother with his lawsuit on his golf-course lot. And this time the stakes were higher. These suits were for $113,000 apiece. I knew there was no escrow hold-back, I knew the number was valid, and I knew I did not have $113,000 hiding under my mattress. I couldn't help hoping that maybe the IRS still owed me something.

I started by calling the bank's attorney and asking if we could negotiate a settlement prior to going to court so I would not have to hire an attorney. Thankfully, they said that was acceptable, and I began to negotiate the settlements on my own. It took five months, but the final amount that I ended up having to pay out of pocket was $5,770, and it didn't have to be paid until December 2009. This was nothing short of the hand of God intervening in my life. I certainly possessed no negotiating skills against a trained attorney, and I held no bargaining chip. I had nothing to bring to the table but a group of prayer warriors. But prayer was all I needed. My brother Jeff was able to get his amount greatly reduced as well.

October 2, 2008

I continued to meet with Tammy, Robin, and now Robin's mom, Irene, for Bible study and prayer time. On October 2, we were in the middle of our prayer time, which sometimes lasted an hour, when my right leg began to jump, much like when you are very nervous and your leg bounces up and down. But I was not nervous, and the jumping soon moved to my left leg as well. Both of my shoes were bouncing quietly off the carpet, making a slight noise as they made contact with the table leg. Our prayers continued. Soon both my arms started to twitch, until I was shaking like a leaf.

Sweating and unable to control the tremors, I was so glad when the prayers finished so I could ask for a glass of water. By now the other women had noticed my unusual movements, so as soon as I drank my water, they anointed me with oil, laid hands on me, and lifted up mighty prayers on my behalf. It made no difference to them that we had already been praying for over an hour.

Irene and Robin spoke over me, both in English and in tongues. Though I could not understand the words in tongues, I was so grateful to have these two prayer warriors on my side. God's presence was always in the room with us on Wednesday nights, and this evening was no exception. Forty-five minutes later, the prayers and tremors had subsided, and I was able to drive home.

The music was still playing in my head, and I heard it that night, as I did most nights. Sometimes I heard it during the day too, but it was especially clear at night and almost nonstop whenever I was trying to go to sleep. I hoped I was not going crazy.

During this time, I was also learning more about the Holy Spirit, and I was on a search to better understand the baptism of the Holy Spirit. Robin answered many of my questions and gave me several books to read. I found the whole topic fascinating.

October 6

Let me share with you a prayer I prayed just a few days later that reflected the attitude of my heart:

Dear Heavenly Father,

I come to You this morning with praise. You are a mighty God. You are in control, You are the answer, and You are everything. I look at the coming day and know that You have brought the sun forth from night—the colors of the sky, the coolness of the morning air. I thank You for that. Lord, I also praise you for a good night's sleep. I know this is a gift from You. I know that my body and mind are restored, healed, and refreshed by You during this time. Thank You.

Lord, the world seems to be quickly flying out of control. Nations rise against other nations, and people rise against other people. It is all very scary to me. The last days are supposed to be ones of rejoicing in Your coming, and although I do rejoice in that, the events leading to that time are unsettling. With so many angry and frightened people all around, the world seems like it is spinning out of control. I know that I intentionally do not think about these things, and I know that I avoid listening to the news and talk radio. I am sorry, Lord, that I am so fearful. Please take my fear and help me to trust You more, as I know You are in control of everything.

I thank You for the healing You have provided. I am beginning to feel like I am coming out of the grieving process. The first round of properties is almost gone. The fear and embarrassment are passing. Thank You for providing such strong support for me during the past two years. I still would like to figure out how You can use me and this situation to help others. Help me to see You and Your path. Continue to heal my mind, soul, and spirit. Anoint the scars with your soothing oil.

Lord, it would be so easy to become bitter, so easy to live a life unto myself only, so easy to take revenge, and so easy to hate. I pray that You will keep me from all of this. Put in my heart forgiveness for others even though they did me wrong. Put in my heart love that I may continue to show Your love to others.

Lord, I do not want to fall into that category of desperate people who do desperate things. It would be easy, but please keep me above that. Lord, I pray for a new vision, a new dream, a new goal. I pray that You would keep me in the center of Your will, that You would use me in such a way that only Your name would be glorified.

Lord, I give You everything I have: my marriage, my finances, my retirement, my family, my expenses, my debt, my properties, my business. Everything I lay at Your feet. Teach me. Guide me. Direct me.

Lord, I also lift up Kim to you. I love him so much. He is going through the same struggles as I am, with the loss of everything. I am sorry that at times I forget he is also suffering. I pray that Your peace would be with him. Help me to put his feelings and needs above my own and to be the wife he needs for me to be. Lord, I want him to be able to trust You and know that You will never fail him.

Lord, today I ask that You would reveal Your gift to me. Help me to find it, to use it, and to let others see You in me. Let everyone that I come into contact with see You and Your goodness, not me and my selfish ways. I am Your child, and I am so grateful for all that You have done for me. For all the answered prayers, thank You, Lord—thank You for everything. May Your name be glorified, and today may my life be lived in the way You would have me live it. Amen.

October 23

Towards the end of October, I noticed that I was at peace much more of the time. I was not spending my time in a state of panic or worrying over everything. If something did not get paid, I was okay with it. Slowly I was learning to lean on God for everything. Once I got to sleep each night, I slept well.

November 2008

Much like the "asthma" of a couple of years earlier, the tremors began to occur more and more often. Once they occurred while I was in church. The ushers and medics were great, and in no time flat, I was in an ambulance and headed for the ER. Although I told the staff there that I had seen a doctor about the tremors, there was no stopping them. After conducting several expensive tests in the ER, they were still unable to determine what the problem was.

I started going to different doctors in search of a diagnosis. While trying to determine the cause of the tremors, they discovered that my thyroid was enlarged. So off to an endocrinologist I went. After a couple of tests, including swallowing a radioactive pill, it appeared that I had lesions on my thyroid, and there was a chance they could be cancerous. Though the doctors never did find a cause for the tremors, the search allowed them to discover something else that could have had serious ramifications.

December 11, 2008

On December 11, my mother-in-law passed away unexpectedly. This was yet another loss for our family, especially for my husband.

December 14

A few days later, I wrote to Dr. R., my parents' pastor, to give him an update of what had been going on. Here is the text of that e-mail:

Hi, Dr. R.,

Mom told me that you asked about me the other day. I thought I would give you a quick update, as you have been watching all this unfold from the sidelines since the beginning.

It has been a tough year, but one that I am sure will be life changing in many ways. As you know, I struggled for twenty-two months to keep everything with the business going until I finally depleted all of the business account as well as my personal savings.

After meeting with you in February, I stopped making the payments on the land and a few of the houses. Remarkably, in January I had received six notices from tenants wanting to break their leases. After looking at the numbers, those were the houses that I needed to get rid of first. I am grateful that God provided reasons for them to move without my having to foreclose on the houses and force them out.

I was determined to fold up my business with just as much integrity as I had tried to run it. The next few months were tough. The collection calls became incessant, and each call was a reminder of my failure. I worked very hard to sell the houses on short sales and then worked even harder to get the bank to accept the offers. On a couple of properties, the bank did accept the offers, and we were able to close. On many more, the banks were totally unreasonable and declined the offers. At this point, one house has sold, two properties have gone to foreclosure auction, and six or seven more are in various stages of being foreclosed upon. So that is sort of the status of the business.

At this moment, from a financial aspect, I have lost everything. My entire financial portfolio, including life savings, retirement funds, business, investment properties, life insurance, and even my ability to obtain credit and loans, is gone.

But what is more important is what I am learning and how God is working in the background. I now realize that I had placed my security in all the things that I owned, which I have since lost, rather than in God. But God is all that I need, and I am seeing His handiwork in every aspect of my life. I know without a doubt that He is walking right beside me as I walk through this desert wilderness. I am learning much, not only about business, but additionally about myself and the God I am trying to serve. It is my desire to continue to grow in this knowledge.

At times I feel like the servant who had one talent and buried it in the dirt. God called him lazy and wicked. I feel like I wasted a wonderful opportunity by making some bad decisions, and I pray for another opportunity to be used by God.

Right now, I do not know what the future holds. I still have properties to get rid of, short sales to close on, foreclosures to deal with, and three lawsuits to face. I am in the middle of one suit now and have two more to go through shortly. In addition, I still need to repay four private investors who provided funds for the business. It was my original intent to pay them back with the profits from the sale of the rentals. When that was no longer possible, it was my intent to pay them back from the profits on the commercial deal I was involved in. When that was no longer possible, it was my intent to pay them back, even though it would be slower, with commissions from my traditional real estate business. Although I am blessed and have clients, I am not making enough to pay them back and also pay my own bills. So the only option that Kim and I can see is to sell our primary home, since we still have equity in it. Early next year, we will put it on the market and see what happens.

I will admit, I have mixed feelings over this decision. I do want to meet my obligations, but as Kim and I will be unable to purchase another home for several years, we will be forced to rent. I have always owned my home. It is my prayer that God just opens all the right doors and whatever is supposed to happen does.

For right now, I am continuing with my traditional real-estate agent work. God is blessing me with clients, and although there is more work involved, I am getting some closed transactions. I think I need to finish dismantling the company and then take a deep breath before I try to figure out what is next.

Emotionally, physically, and mentally, I need some time to go through a healing process. I think the past year has been one of great grieving as a result of all the losses, including my grandmother, and only time will get me ready for the next adventure. Thus Psalm 46:10, "Be still and know that I am God," is one of my favorite verses right now. So all in all, I can say I am okay. I can honestly say God has blessed me this year and walked beside me. God is faithful, and every day He surrounds me with His love from friends like you and your wife. Thank you for your prayers and concerns.

Jami

December 15

I decided to attend the women's group at my mom's church. I often attended this group and counted these women among my friends. We were asked to bring a Christmas ornament and then write about the gift that God had given to us this past year. This was my letter:

The gift that God has so generously bestowed upon me this year is the gift of His faithful provision. But in order for me to more fully recognize, understand, and appreciate His gift, I first had to have many things stripped from me. Please allow me to elaborate.

In the past year, my entire financial portfolio has been lost, including my life savings, my retirement funds, my investment properties, my business, and my ability to obtain credit and loans. I have lost both my grandmother and my mother-in-law. I have lost my pride and self-confidence. Yet God remains faithful. He has provided for me over and over again. Here are some of His gifts to me:

- He provides every breath that I take. It was not too long ago that I was reminded of who is the Sustainer of Life. I now fully appreciate and never take breathing for granted.
- He has given me a very supportive husband who is walking this wilderness road beside me.
- He has given me family and friends, including many of you, who love, support, and pray for me.
- He showed His mercy and grace to both my grandma and my mom as He took my grandmother home.
- When fear, panic, and uncertainty overtook my thoughts, He sent my mom to encourage me, listen to me, and sometimes even cry with me.
- At one point, I did not have the money to pay the electric bill. This was a situation that I had never before experienced. The

day before my electricity was to be turned off, He provided a miracle, and we received a tax refund from 2005. It was enough to pay our bills for five months—long enough to make it through the normally slow real estate season.

- He is teaching me that His provision is timed and that my timing and His are not always the same.
- He continues to put a song in my heart and a smile on my lips. By His grace, I still have a sense of humor, and I have not given in to despair or bitterness.

Yes, God is faithful. As I walk through my own desert wilderness, He provides my daily manna.

As December 2008 came to a close, I could look back and gratefully say I had made it through another year. Yes, it was a year filled with great losses, and I can honestly say it was a year when I experienced the hardest time of my life thus far. I closed only ten real estate transactions that year—my worst year ever. But it was also a year that would impact the rest of my life and a year in which God made Himself very evident. For that reason, it was one of my richest years ever, filled with many showers of blessings on my wilderness journey.

10

Year 2009: It Is Raining

January 8, 2009

The tremors were still continuing, and I was scheduled to go in to check my thyroid. I had just finished reading a book on the baptism of the Holy Spirit, and I prayed that God would release His Spirit and let His power be more fully realized in my life. I was not exactly sure what I was praying for, but I knew I had experienced a burning desire to know God more fully for some time now and had been diligently seeking Him.

I also prayed that God would take away all my fears and started to name them one by one: fear of the unknown, fear of the future, fear of the state of the economy, fear of failing health, fear of no longer having a goal or a plan for my life, and fear of things both real and imagined. Then I listed my blessings one by one: my husband, my family, my friends, my church, my home, my material blessings, all the answered prayers, the peace I had found, the breath in my lungs, and many more. I then once again surrendered myself to God.

I know without a doubt that God heard my prayers. That day the tremors left. I then went to the doctor, and he told me that the thyroid lesions were gone as well as any threat of cancer. Praise God again and again! Later that day, while I was praying, I started saying one particular word over and over. I did not know what this word meant, but I soon realized it was the first word of my prayer language. Praise God forevermore!

February 2009

My husband had been doing research on dogs for several weeks now. We had never owned a dog and really had not ever really talked about getting one. But once the decision was made, Kim spent many hours researching to find us the right dog. He first considered a standard-sized schnauzer and then changed his mind to a standard-sized poodle. We looked at many puppies, and Kim talked to various rescue places; but for one reason or another, none of the dogs seemed right for us.

One day while I was out with a client, I got a phone call from Kim. He asked me to bring home some puppy food and maybe a leash. When I got home, instead of a poodle, there was a white German shepherd puppy waiting for me. We named her Gretchen. Gretchen turned out to be the perfect dog for us; she was so smart and easy to train. But most of all, she gave us both something positive and fun in our lives. Yes, even this little puppy was a gift from God.

I began walking Gretchen early every morning, and at times I compared my relationship with God to the relationship I had with Gretchen. I saw God's unconditional love reflected in that puppy. No matter what type of day I was having or what mood I was in, Gretchen was always happy to see me. Whenever I walked into the house, she was always there to greet me with her tail furiously wagging.

Kim and I soon discovered that Gretchen was afraid to ride in the car. So we decided to help her overcome her fear by taking her to dog parks and other places where she could play and have fun. She loved it once she got there, but the ride was hard for her.

Watching Gretchen struggle, I realized how much like her I was. The rides in my life were not fun either, but when I finally arrived at the destination, it was worth it. In all the circumstances of my life, God knew what was best for me. He knew that when I got there, I was going to have fun, but He had to get me into the car and assure me the whole way there that it would be okay. This was exactly what He had been doing for the past three years of my life: *It will be okay. It will be fun. Life is going to be better. Hang on; there's a little bump. Here is a treat to encourage you while we drive. Stop being fearful; I am here.* How long would I have to keep going on car rides to learn to stop fighting change?

Gretchen also did not like to be left alone. She preferred to keep her "pack" in sight and to stay very close to either my husband or me. She would roam from room to room looking for us and sleep in the doorway of whichever room we were in.

One day while I was out, I realized again how much like Gretchen I was. I pondered the times when I had left Gretchen alone at home while I went out on an errand. I did not forget about her while I was gone, and I was out of sight for only a short period of time. I knew she was fine, and I knew she was safe, even if she didn't realize it.

At times in my life, however, I had felt just like Gretchen, as though God had left me alone in the wilderness. At those times, it indeed seemed like He was out of sight. But the truth was, He was constantly thinking of me; though He was out of my sight, I was never out of His sight. He never leaves us. Once more, I was reminded of the words of Scripture and encouraged by them: "Be strong and courageous. Do not be afraid or terrified because of them, for the Lord your God goes with you; he will never leave you nor forsake you" (Deut. 31:6).

March 2009

By this point, I was running out of ideas on how to pay back my private investors. Originally they were to be paid from the sale of the rental properties, but that idea failed. Then I was going to pay them out of the proceeds from the commercial lot; that idea also failed. By now I was pretty much out of assets, yet I felt that it was very important to get the investors paid off. I knew they all needed the money.

Back in December, my husband had suggested that we sell our home. I struggled with the idea for a while. We had custom built our home; it was exactly the way we liked it. Plus, with the foreclosures and short sales on our credit, we would have to rent if we sold our home.

I think the idea of renting was the hardest part for me. From dealing with so many tenants, I now had a sour taste in my mouth towards renting. Of course, I had caused part of my financial problems, but I had also lost quite a bit of money directly related to issues with tenants. I really did not want to be one. I recognized this as a pride issue, but I so desperately wanted to hold on to some dignity. Nevertheless, we listed the house, knowing that paying off our debt was a good thing and this was probably the only way we could do that. But hadn't we just gotten a puppy? Talk about timing!

I was still working at getting rid of the properties. It usually takes a minimum of six months from the time when you stop making payments for a property to go to trustee sale. In order to lessen the hit against my credit, I tried to do short sales on all of them. A short sale is when you negotiate with the bank to accept a sales price that is less than what is owed on the property. Because it takes the bank eight to twelve weeks to process the file, the six months often gets pushed back. That is great news if you are living in the house rent free, but it is not so great if you still have to maintain the property and pay HOA dues.

As we tried to get rid of the properties, Kim and I were simultaneously cleaning and marketing our house for sale. Though people looked at it almost every week, we got no offers. We continued to lower the price.

The music, too, was still playing in my head. For the first time, I asked God what this music was, and although I did not hear an audible voice, I felt impressed with the thought *I am protecting your mind.* So was this the reason that I had been able to get through much of 2008 and endure all the losses without dropping into a deep state of depression? I had prayed specifically for His protection from depression, and He answered that prayer in a truly remarkable way.

Since the day of that realization, I have not heard the music again. But I am comforted to know that He was actively engaged in protecting my mind and spirit from all the negative thoughts and emotions that could easily have stolen my joy, peace, and hope. To Him be the glory!

July 2009

I sold the very first house that I had purchased with Next Step Properties, LLC. I had acquired it outright from another investor back in 2002, and it was the perfect model for the lease-option program. The house, which was completely handicapped accessible, was uniquely suited to the tenant. She had a son in a wheelchair, so the house was perfect for them.

The tenant had been in the house for seven years and was finally in a position to obtain her own financing. Originally, when she moved into the house, her credit did not allow her to purchase the home.

Medical bills had hurt her financial standing, but she did have a very good job. She paid me fifteen thousand dollars when she moved in and then paid fourteen hundred dollars a month. My monthly payment on the house was only twelve hundred dollars, so it was actually a positive cash-flowing property for me. This tenant's rent payment was always on time, and she never called with complaints. I never saw the inside of the house after I gave her the keys.

In the beginning, we agreed on a specific purchase price, and I received fifteen thousand dollars of my profit when she moved in. I walked away from the closing with an additional fifty-seven hundred dollars, just enough to cover the deficiency judgment on the golf course lot. Isn't it amazing how the numbers always work out?

August 2009

I attended a business training meeting, and the speaker talked of a ninety-day run in which you keenly focus on business and put all your energy into the necessary tasks for ninety days. I decided to take the challenge.

My business was doing okay, and I had five solid clients under contract. These contracts would provide just enough funds to pay my bills for the remainder of the year. However, I still had the four investors that I needed to pay off. I decided to really focus on my marketing and do everything I could in order to increase my business and allocate all the extra commissions towards my private investors. To do this, I would need approximately fifteen additional transactions. Knowing that this would not be an easy task or one that I could handle alone, I prayed about the situation.

On August 15, I sent this prayer request to my prayer team:

It appears that God is not going to sell our house at this time. We have not had any showings in three weeks, and the sales flyers are staying in the box longer. If that changes, then so be it. But I still have an obligation to repay my debts. I want to honor my promise, and I feel that anything less than full payment is unacceptable.

It is my belief, through the Word of God, that it is His desire that I be out of debt. I have seen His mighty provision many times, especially in the past two years. I have seen God provide a million dollars four times in less than thirty days. I have seen Him marvelously and wonderfully provide when there was no other way. I am a witness and a beneficiary of His love.

With that in mind, I am laying at His feet my five fish and two breadsticks. I come before Him with only my mind, my energy, my enthusiasm, my knowledge, and my desire to have His name glorified by this blessing. I am praying that God would provide a hundred thousand dollars in commissions above and beyond the five transactions I am currently working on. This is impossible in my own power, but I am running on the power of the Holy Spirit for the next ninety days. He will provide the strength, the clients, the contracts, the closings, and the commissions. All of this extra income will be used to pay off my investors. I will keep none of the funds.

I ask that you lift up this request as I once again watch Jehovah-Jireh provide a blessing not only to me but also to those who blessed me several years back with the lending of their resources.

Jami

I decided that during this time, I needed to sacrifice something to God and not just focus all my energy on real estate. So I decided to abstain from all beverages except for water for the next ninety days. That meant no milk on my cereal, no coffee in the morning, no diet Coke when my nerves were shot. I also decided that I should extend this run to conclude with Thanksgiving. So now my ninety days became a hundred days.

I began by praying that God would be glorified during this time and that I would have a closer walk with Him. I also asked for unprecedented favor for my business. Then I started marketing. I sent out postcards, and I teamed up with a lender who had a great plan to market to teachers. I called my past client database and even met with a sales coach. I did all the things that should make a difference and give me a great fourth quarter.

But the phones remained quiet. I was busy baby-sitting the five escrows I had, making sure they went through, but each of them, for one reason or another, was delayed. Closings that should have happened in mid- September got pushed back to October. Again there was no money in the bank, and again the bills were sitting on the desk waiting for manna from heaven.

In the midst of all this, I did, however, have a peace and assurance that God was in control. I was not anxious, but I was curious about the way things were working out and watched with anticipation as events unfolded. It seemed I was in the middle of a battle. As soon as I thought I had a new contract, it was canceled, but then another client would step in to replace that one, only to cancel also. On four occasions, contracts were accepted and then canceled. I still had the original five transactions, which when they closed would just cover my bills. God was providing just enough—no more, no less.

During the time when this tug-of-war was going on, several other situations arose that could have discouraged me and possibly derailed my hundred-day run, but instead, they just provided additional opportunities for God to show His everlasting grace and mercy as He continued to rain His love along my path. Here are some of the things that happened during that hundred-day period of time:

1. On August 20, 2009, I received an e-mail regarding a change in the deficiency law. Effective September 30, 2009, I would be responsible for the deficiencies on the remaining four rental properties. These properties were houses, which had previously been exempt from deficiency paybacks— but no more. Altogether they would cost me

between four hundred thousand and five hundred thousand dollars.

Many of my clients, also with rental properties, were nervous about this new law, as was I. I started learning as much as I could about it and how it might impact us. The Arizona Association of Realtors, as well as several attorneys, were all lobbying to get this bill repealed. I spoke to various attorneys and attended meetings regarding the issue. There really was no loophole for us. All I could do was to put it in God's hands. Three times before, He had mercifully allowed the deficiency lawsuits to be manageable, so I trusted He would do the same thing again. I slept in peace.

On September 12, 2009, the law was overturned with the passing of the state budget. This was a miracle in and of itself because the budget itself was very controversial, and only a last-minute provision added to the budget repealed this bill. We would not face any additional lawsuits. Hallelujah!

2. My husband's computer crashed, forcing him to buy a new one. Where would we get the funds to pay for it? We received a check in the mail from Volkswagen for car repairs we had paid for on a recalled item. The check covered the cost of the new PC. Another summer mist drifted down on us.

3. October rolled around. Three of the escrows were closed, and the last two were due to

close shortly. But my phone hardly ever rang, and I went an entire weekend with no client appointments. It was strange; this had never happened before. But I was at peace, the peace that comes only from God. I slept well at night, knowing that God was at work.

4. My car's check-engine light began coming on. We took the vehicle in, and the mechanics decided that it was probably the transmission. However, they started by just changing the fluid, and we got by with only a four-hundred-dollar bill.

   Additionally, an old investment we thought was lost forever finally paid out. We received a check for six hundred dollars, a big loss from the initial investment but enough to cover the car repairs.

5. Another slow week drew to an end, and I went to lunch with my friend Nancy. As I left the restaurant, my car overheated and the check-engine light came back on. After having the vehicle towed to the garage, I was told that several items needed attention, including a new transmission. The estimate was $5,875, money Kim and I did not have. Searching for funds, I discovered an old stock account buried deep in the back of the file cabinet and cashed it in. That brought in three thousand dollars. I had three thousand dollars left on my last credit card, so I decided to use that for the difference.

The transmission needed to be ordered, and it would take some time to come in, so we decided to rent a car for the weekend. That would provide me with transportation if I needed to meet with clients. The next weekend, I attempted to rent another car, only to discover that my credit card had been canceled. Not this again! I thought we were through with that kind of humiliation.

I walked out of the building, somewhat embarrassed and a little defeated. Now how were we going to pay for the transmission? I laid this matter at God's feet, along with everything else. The pile of things I was trusting Him for was ever growing.

6. Another extremely quiet weekend was upon me, so I decided to take advantage of it. My husband was at a weekend meeting, I had no appointments, and I had no car; so I relaxed, cleaned the house, did laundry, read, and prayed. It was such a great weekend. I even skipped church, as I wanted the quiet time alone. My spirit was refreshed, and my mind felt relaxed. I had the thought to write a book to remind myself of all the times and ways God has blessed me, and I started on it.

7. A friend of mine gave me a spiritual-gifts assessment book from his church. I took the test and scored high in encouragement, faith, and mercy. I guess it was that mercy gift that got me in trouble with being a land-lord. Looking back, I can see that I was far

too lenient with the tenants and gave them the benefit of the doubt far too many times before evicting them for nonpayment.

8. In the midst of all our problems, my husband and I were drawing closer together. My heart was softened in some areas, and we were a stronger couple in our relationship than we had been in a long time.

9. My prayer one morning was that God would provide the means for me to pay for my car repairs and would give me a sign of encouragement that I should stay in real estate. *Does God want me in another place doing something else?* I wondered. The total lack of new clients was a little unsettling, and I wondered if He was trying to tell me to move forward with something else.

I did have a closing later that day, one of the original five, and I was grateful for it. The clients originally had a certain home under contract; however, after many months, the contract fell apart. Then they found another wonderful home for less money. After we finished all the paperwork, my clients handed me a check, facedown, and told me that it was laid on their hearts to give this to me. I insisted that it was not necessary and explained that I got paid through the transaction. But they insisted in turn that they wanted to do this, aware that I had lost some commission with their purchase of the lower-priced home. I truly appreciated the thought, but I felt bad about accepting the check.

I slowly turned the check over and saw it was for twenty-five hundred dollars! I was speechless, not only for the amount of the "tip," but because I knew this was an answer to my morning prayer. I could now pay for my car! *Is this also the sign of encouragement I asked for in sticking with this job?* My head was filled with so many thoughts that I did not know what to say. I hurried home to tell my husband of this latest blessing, and just an hour later, the garage called to say my car was ready for pickup. What a big downpour of blessing!

10. My prayer to know more of God continued to be answered. While helping with the church bulletins one day, I was invited to join a women's Bible study. Bible Study Fellowship is an in-depth study that lasts eight years; this year's study was on the Gospel of John.

11. A friend from church, Lynette, whom I had been encouraging with her real estate business, asked me if I would like to meet once a week to pray about our businesses. I was very excited with the prospect because Lynette was very grounded in the Word and had spent the last twenty-five years teaching Bible studies. During our time together, I am sure I learned much more from her than she learned about real estate from me. This godly woman helped

bring me to a much deeper understanding of God's Word, His Spirit, and His power.

12. On October 20, during one of my prayer sessions with Lynette, God's power was released in me in a new way: I received more of my prayer language! It was such an awesome experience.

First, Lynette had me stand up and lift my hands in an act of submission. Then she put her hands on my shoulders and prayed for me to receive the baptism of the Holy Spirit and the release of God's power in my life. She then started speaking in the Spirit. After a few minutes, she told me to try to mimic her. I tried, but the sounds coming from my mouth sounded much different from hers, though almost as fluent.

After a few minutes, we stopped and sat down together. Then Lynette told me to pray again in my prayer language so I would be encouraged. I did, and the heavenly language came just as easily as before. After a couple of minutes, one of my legs started to shake. I spoke out loud, "No fear, no fear!" and the trembling stopped.

A very peaceful feeling swept over me. I can only equate the feeling to the same thing that I experienced at the time of my paternal grandmother's death in 1997: I just knew I was in the presence of God. I was so excited to receive this new gift from above and eagerly desired to know more of God. Every day after that, I prayed in my prayer language, still amazed by the wonder of it.

The next week when Lynette and I met, we prayed both in English and in the Spirit. As we prayed, all four of my limbs started to tremble. I mentioned to Lynette that I had not experienced the tremors since January, except on these last two occasions with her. We prayed that my body would come into submission and that the devil would not gain a foothold with fear. The tremors did not return again.

That marked a turning point for me in my spiritual development. I realized that much as I have a choice between having a positive attitude towards life or a negative one, I have the choice between letting fear dominate my life or walking in faith. Both are conscious decisions on how I will react to life's events. That day I chose to live in faith, and that has been my choice ever since!

Never in forty-five years had I had such strong Christian women, like Lynette, surrounding me. This was such a tremendous blessing that I was almost afraid that it would not last.

End of October 2009

I had not had any new clients since August 15. Although a couple of clients were looking at properties, nothing new was under contract, and no one new was calling. Yet, I had peace; I was okay.

The verse "Seek first his kingdom and his righteousness, and all these things will be given to you as well" (Matt. 6:33) came to my mind during a morning walk one day. At that moment, it dawned on me that this one hundred day period was not going to be about real estate but instead an answer to my other prayer of getting closer to God.

Each new week brought new blessings and joys. On Monday nights, I attended the Bible Study Fellowship class and was always spiritually charged when I left. I often prayed in the parking lot and on my way home, rejoicing that God was present and marveling in some new revelation. There was such joy in my spirit that I had a hard time sleeping.

But there was no time to sleep in, as Tuesday mornings brought me to my study time with Lynette. With much anticipation, I looked forward to each of these meetings. Although Lynette's knowledge and insight were sometimes more than a little intimidating to me, I knew I was supposed to be at those meetings. I never had any idea what our topic of conversation would be, but I did know it would not be real estate for long.

Every Tuesday I left Lynette's house so on fire for God. I knew I was not grasping all that she was teaching me, but she was so gracious and allowed me to take baby steps. After my Tuesday morning meeting with Lynette, I will admit that the rest of the day was not a very productive workday for me. My mind seemed to whirl a hundred miles an hour all day and well into the night. But it was well worth it, and I was more than grateful for the experience.

Every other Wednesday, Tammy, Robin, and a couple of other women continued to meet for our study. We often cut our time short after three hours or so. Our prayer time was always powerful, and we all saw so many answered prayers. So on those days, I again went to bed with a joyful spirit and found myself praising God well into the night. These were more than gentle rain showers—they were downpour blessings!

November 3, 2009

This Tuesday, as every Tuesday, I went to my prayer meeting with Lynette. After we prayed about our businesses, she asked if she could pray for me. *Didn't we just finish up fifteen minutes of prayer?* I thought. But I never say no to prayer, so I agreed to her request.

Lynette placed her hands on my shoulders and began to pray in the Spirit. Her hands were hot. As she prayed, I did not have any specific thoughts going through my mind, but I did feel a sense of peace and noticed that her hands were hot. Then she moved one of her hands to the middle of my back and prayed for about five more minutes. When she finished, she asked whether I had any sensations or thoughts to share. Sheepish, I felt like maybe I should have been trying harder while she prayed, but I had to admit that I only felt a sense of peace and submission and was very relaxed. I had not known this was a test.

Then Lynette said she had a word for me. She shared that God had many gifts for me and that I should open them. She stated that He had given me the gift of faith and healing miracles for me to use for others. I had not told her about the spiritual-assessment test I had taken. No one except my mom knew I had taken that test. When I asked Lynette what I should do with this gift and what my next steps should be, she encouraged me to pray about it.

It was a good thing I was not busy with real estate, as there was no way I could have focused on work for the rest of the day after this encounter.

From that point on, however, I did exactly what Lynette had advised me to do. On a daily basis, I prayed to hear God's Spirit speaking to me and to possess the ability to recognize it as His, discern it correctly, and then act on it.

November 9

For some reason, I started the day with the idea that this day, 11/9/09, was the first day of the rest of my life. It seemed appropriate, however, since my life had changed so drastically eight years ago on 9/11/01. The correlation of the numbers somehow seemed significant.

Nothing specific was happening in my life, yet I awakened that morning knowing this statement, that today was the first day of the rest of my life, to be true. As I pondered, I realized that this hundred-day run, much like the commercial project, had been predicated on my sensing that I needed to take some sort of action and come before almighty God. In both cases, I was not sure why I felt that way and thus assumed that it must be about real estate, but that was never the case. It was never about my investors, and it was

145

never about my getting out of debt. It was always about bringing me to a point of total submission so that I could be open to the Word and the Spirit of God. It was so I would have the desire to hear Him and act on His promptings. I had no idea where I was going from here, but I knew without a doubt that I was headed in a new direction!

November 10

At Lynette's this day, I gained some additional insights on communion and the word *faith*. Lynette also encouraged me to be aware of the promptings of the Spirit.

November 12

I did not have many appointments that day and felt the need to be by myself. I decided to fast for twenty-four hours, and after dealing with a few items, I went to the church to pray and study. I had been there for awhile when I suddenly realized that for the first time in a very long time, I did not have a crisis that I needed to pray about. My mind was quiet; I was not upset, worried, or torn about anything. It was very comforting to realize that some real healing had occurred in the past few months—emotionally, mentally, physically, and spiritually.

Nothing on the outside had changed. I still had no clients; I still had no idea how to pay back my investors; I still had no more financial resources than before. I was still praying daily for my daily bread, but it was truly okay. I sat there for three hours, reading, praying some, but mainly just enjoying the quietness around and within me.

November 13

God's rain clouds were gathering, though I did not know it. At 4:00 p.m., I received a call from one of my previous clients, asking me to list her rental property for sale. This was my first new client in a long time. I went back and counted the days from August 15 to November 13, and it was ninety days exactly. Don't tell me God does not have a sense of humor and perfect timing!

My prayer to get closer to Him was answered in a huge and awesome way. He provided me with the time that I needed to start on this new journey and now was providing me with my daily bread. Yes, when I initially had the thought to seek Him first and then "all these things will be added to you," I had been right on track.

The rain clouds continued to gather that same evening. I had purchased a book on prayer several months earlier, but it had sat on the shelf unopened. I had actually forgotten about it. That evening around eight, I had a desire to read and searched for something to occupy my time before going to bed. I picked up the long-neglected book and started reading it. Entitled *Authority in Prayer,*[7] it was written by Dutch Sheets, and I was absolutely blown away by it.

I had spent the last two years learning about living a victorious life. I had been reading God's Word and listening to Robin and Irene pray. I had been a diligent student of God and His ways. But it was not until this night that I discovered what I had been searching for.

How do I live a victorious life in my everyday world? had been my long-standing question. No one had been able to answer it in a manner that I could get my head around. Okay, I am a slow study. I admit, I have only two brain cells, and most of the time, they are tired. But how to put victorious Christian living into consistent practice had eluded me up to this point.

The book explained that God has all the power, yet He has given us the authority to use His power in our everyday lives. We have been given permission, or authority, to access His power in our lives. Like the proverbial light bulb going on, I realized that *authority* was what made Robin's prayers so powerful. That was the difference. She had the God- given authority to ask for change, and she exercised it, knowing that God would back her with His power. This was a totally new insight for me, but with it, so many things started to make sense. No wonder Robin's prayers sounded so confident. They were! Her faith allowed her to go to the throne of grace with confidence that her prayers were in alignment with the Father's will.

Surely someone somewhere had explained this to me before. But my mind must have been blinded or was not ready to accept this truth until now, the ninetieth day of my search for a closer walk with God. What a wonderful, awesome gift to end this day and week on! This truly was the first week of the rest of my life, and I eagerly waited for the next week to begin.

God was at work in my life in a very powerful and awesome way. I had no idea where we were going, but I knew it would be a grand adventure. For the first time in twenty-five years, my desire to excel in a job, be a successful business owner, or earn a six-figure income was nothing compared to what I was experiencing that evening. I prayed that I could remain this close to God for the rest of my life. If chapter 1 held such revelation for me, maybe I needed to read the rest of the book!

November 22

Kim and I were driving around the airport waiting to pick up our friends who were visiting for the week when I received a call from someone who was sitting by the only realty sign I had in the field. He asked if I could help him buy several investment properties, but there was a catch. He was from Colorado, so we would have to complete the transactions this week before Friday morning. I agreed to meet with him early Monday morning.

November 26

It was Thanksgiving Day, or in my case, day 100. I awoke with a heart full of gratitude and joy. It was a beautiful day in Phoenix. A clear blue sky was above me, and a song was on my lips. I was truly grateful for my opportunity to walk in the wilderness and even more thankful for the past hundred days. In all my wilderness wanderings, God had not left me for even one day. Not once had He let me down. Not once had

He withheld His blessings from me. Rather, He had provided more than I could ever have imagined.

Never would I have asked for this time in the wilderness; never would I have asked for a time of such great loss; but without it, never would my life have been so changed. God allowed me to endure some hardships and showed Himself faithful. Each time the test got harder, but each time He was faithful. My faith was stretched and strengthened until I was no longer the same. *Thank You, Lord, for everything, but mostly for Your everlasting love,* sang my heart.

Working at my desk later in the evening, I leaned back in my chair and gazed at the plaque on my wall, the one with my life verse on it, Jeremiah 29:11: "For I know the plans I have for you," declares the Lord, "plans to prosper you and not to harm you, plans to give you hope and a future." I decided to look the verse up in my Bible lying beside me. I read it aloud, putting my name in all the places that say "you": "For I know the plans I have for Jami," declares the Lord, "plans to prosper Jami and not to harm Jami, plans to give Jami a hope and a future." I continued reading the next two verses: "Then Jami will call upon me and come and pray to me, and I will listen to Jami. Jami will seek me and find me when Jami seeks me with all her heart. I will be found by Jami." I am sure I had read verses 12–13 before, but that night, for the first time, my verse was saying something completely different to me. I had called upon Him, and I had indeed sought Him; and true to His word, I found something far more precious than silver or gold, a heavenly treasure of infinitely greater value.

With my hundred-day challenge drawing to a close, I sent an update to my prayer partners:

November 26, 2009

To my prayer team:

Well, I cannot say that the last hundred days were not eventful. I know this time has changed my life forever, even though I am not certain of all the ways right now. I have made some significant progress on my desire to get closer to God. On November 13 (day 90), I had zero business in my pipeline. However, in the last ten days, I have added six new transactions that hopefully will all close by the year's end.

Per my commitment, any commissions from this activity will be used to pay off my investors. Though this will not completely pay off my debt, it a good start, and I know God will continue to show Himself to be faithful to this end.

I thank you for your prayers and for holding me accountable during this time. By the way, my glass of milk at Thanksgiving dinner and the wine later in the evening were delicious!

Jami

December 1, 2009

I had missed my Bible study meeting that week because I was working. Since I had not really worked for ninety days, as soon as the opportunity presented itself, I ran with it. Sure, I could claim that I needed to work; after all, I had not had a client in ninety days. I could say my client was insistent that we meet and write contracts, and I could defend myself by pointing out that the property probably would not be on the market for long. All of those statements were true, but what I needed to remind myself was that I had already worked all day, giving my client my undivided attention for eight hours. Now I needed to take time out for God. I needed to go to the mountain for rest and prayer. I needed to learn more about the things that last longer than a paycheck. That's what I should have done, but I did not.

So there I was, reading the notes on John 6 a week late. Verse 27 said, "Do not work for food that spoils, but for food that endures to eternal life, which the Son of Man will give you." The discussion notes read, "Cease to direct the whole effort of your life into seeking material gain and temporary satisfaction." The words *whole effort* hit me hard. I willingly and freely admitted to myself that I enjoyed working. I was a workaholic. I knew this, and my family and friends knew it too. To me, it was not about the money, but the challenge and satisfaction of a job well done.

I thought back on the last hundred days. None of it had been a fluke or a coincidence. God had laid everything out exactly as it needed to be. I had asked for signs large enough to be seen by someone as literal and dense as me, and I did see. One hundred days—the first ninety were given to me so that I could be quiet, so that I could spend time and energy on getting closer to God. At the end of that period, ten days were given for me to work.

This was not the normal 10 percent tithe of the firstfruits to God and the remaining 90 percent for me, but a complete reversal. I had given God more: more of my time, more of my life, more of my energy. In the process, I had found satisfaction in Him, which was truly what I was seeking.

Suddenly I remembered the three trash bags from my grandmother's room after her death. True satisfaction, true meaning, and true eternity—these were the things I wanted my earthly life to stand for. I was deep in thought: *Can I truly change? Do I truly want to change? If I do, how do I start? How do I practically put into practice Matthew 6:33: "Seek ye first the kingdom of God, and his righteousness; and all these things shall be added unto you"?* (KJV).

11

Year 2010: The Desert Blooms

My wilderness walk was drawing to an end. I sensed I was nearing an oasis ahead. I had waited for this for four long years, yet I moved slowly, not running towards it and forgetting the past as I had planned. No, I did not want to forget the past. I did not want to forget the lessons learned, both in business and in my spiritual life. I did not want to ever lose the new closeness I felt with God. I did not want to get distracted by my own ambitions.

No, I did not want to forget the pain, the provision, and the blessings. I did not want to forget how my husband, my family, and my friends had rallied and supported me when I was at my lowest. I wanted to change and continue to grow, but to forget would make the last four years a waste. No, I did not want to ever forget.

For a long time, I had felt that my story was not just for me alone. In some way, I believed God wanted to use it to reach others with His love, comfort, peace, and hope. He loves each of us in a very special and real way. His arms are wide open as He runs towards us, calling to each of us, "My child."

As I thought on all I had been through, in my mind I could picture myself holding several little Monopoly houses and hotels. Each house had the name of one of my rentals: Danbury, Canyon Creek, Thirty-fifth Avenue, Wacker, Fargo, Adams, Papago, etc., and I was holding them so tightly that my hand was bleeding. Little drops of blood dripped from my hand, but still I held on tightly.

Then slowly I relaxed my hand just a little, then a little bit more. With my other hand, I began taking the little blood-covered houses and laying them down on the ground. I continued to release each little house with much love and care until they were all gone from my clenched fist. Then I proceeded to lay down other things that I was still holding onto tightly: my pride, my plans, my finances, my FICO score, my self-confidence.

My hand was now empty and open, palm up, and God was filling it with love, peace, the ability to trust Him, strong Christian friends, an increasingly victorious life, continual provision, true empathy, complete healing, a supportive husband, a loving family, miracle blessings, a stronger testimony, humility, and a new vision for my life. Though the future was not yet fully defined, the groundwork was there. As I relinquished everything I had, God gave me everything I needed. I know it sounds like a cliché, but it is true.

As I write this today, I can truthfully say, so many times God has heard my cry. So many times He has reached down and comforted me. So many times He has provided just what I needed. Maybe it was just a little unexpected check in the mail, but it was always just the amount needed. It was never a day early or a day late. So many times He put the right people, the right circumstances, the right finances in my hand. So many times He used a song on the radio or a kind word from someone to encourage me. Whatever the method, His concern and care were always so abundant.

Some would ask, was it all worth it? Was losing a net worth of five million dollars worth it? The number staggers me, even now, and the entire amount consisted of hard assets, not just paper losses. But would I do it all over again? I honestly would have to answer, "Yes!"

Because of what I went through, my spiritual growth has been unprecedented. My husband and I have survived, and we both have seen how God provides in such a wonderful and obvious way that there can be no denying where it came from. Will we always see God in such a visual way? Perhaps not, but God is the same yesterday, today, and tomorrow. He loves us even if we cannot see Him. We just have to remember that the ride is always worth it in the end, and who knows where this ride will end? Maybe it will be the big dog park.

May you, my readers, have renewed strength as you travel through your wilderness, and may you see the pillar by night and the cloud by day of the all-loving, ever-present God who is leading you. Remember to look for His gentle rain showers of blessings that are ever present, and don't forget to count them one by one.

Here is a song that spoke to me and that I hope will encourage you in your own wilderness journey:

Jesus Calling
By 33 Miles[8]

> What do you see when you look at
> your world today?
> Is it so full of clutter that you feel like
> you're going insane?
> And you can't fight back 'cause
> you're just too afraid
> And it seems like the clouds in
> your sky don't wanna change
>
> You see there's always another story,
> another side to every coin
> And how you see your circumstance
> is all about a choice

CHORUS
> When you see the rushing wind,
> feel the pouring rain
> Hear the thunder now as the clouds roll in
> You're blinded by the lightning
> Do you also hear that still, small voice saying?

"It's okay you're not alone
You may be scared to death but I won't
let you go"
You may think the sky above is falling
But can you hear Jesus calling?

What do you see when you look at
your world today?
Do you see a glimmer of hope, or has it
all turned to gray?
Well, start by counting your blessings one by one
And I'm sure right there, you'll start
to see the sun

You see there's always another story,
another side to every coin
And how you see your circumstance
is all about a choice

CHORUS
Oh, calling out to you
Because the darker the night, the brighter
He can shine

CHORUS
He's calling, He's calling
Calling out to you

May 1, 2010

During my morning prayer time, I stopped to reflect upon the past four months. I recalled how in December 2009, I had asked myself if I truly wanted to change my life and my ways. I had said that I did, but words and actions do not always match. In this case, had my words and desires been followed by appropriate actions?

I thought hard about some of the changes that had occurred. First, I had committed myself not to work on Sundays, one of my busiest days as a realtor. To solidify this commitment to both my clients and to myself, I had changed my message on my cell phone to state this fact, and I left the phone on vibrate during the day on Sundays. Some Sundays I did need to follow up on items, as sometimes there were deadlines involved, but all in all, I was making huge strides in doing only necessary items on Sunday afternoons.

In addition, I was getting up a half hour earlier in the mornings so that I could have more time for study and prayer. Last and most important, God had miraculously given me a change in my attitude towards work. It really was no longer the passion of my life. My family and friends were starting to notice this change in me as well.

May 10

A good friend of mine, who graciously proofread the manuscript, told me that I needed a summary, a conclusion, or a bow to tie it all together. For months, I pondered what that bow would look like. No words came until the night of May 10. That night was the last evening for my Bible Study Fellowship class. We had completed our study on the book of John. I had been deeply touched and moved by the class, and I had learned a great deal and gained many new insights. Tonight, at our final meeting, the bow was provided.

We were studying John 21, where Christ calls to Peter and several other disciples while they are fishing and asks if they have caught anything. They reply that they have not, and Jesus tells them to throw their nets on the other side of the boat. They do, and they catch so many fish that they fear their nets may break.

The disciples come ashore, and Jesus prepares breakfast for them. Then He questions Peter on whether he really loves Him. Three times the Lord asks Peter about his love for Him. Just a few short days earlier, Peter had three times denied even knowing the Lord.

The summary for the lecture on John 21 was short: Peter was refilled, restored, and refocused. First, Peter was refilled both physically and spiritually. After a long night of fishing, his physical needs were met with a breakfast of fish and bread. He was refilled spiritually by spending time with Jesus in unhurried fellowship.

Second, Peter was restored. Peter's position, after his earlier seeming failure, was publicly restored. By questioning Peter's love and demanding that Peter examine his own life, Jesus forced Peter to honestly consider whether he could say he loved the Lord more than he loved anyone or anything else. Peter, in front of his friends, could not state that he loved the Lord in the same way as the Lord loved him, but he did love Jesus to the best of his ability at that moment.

Third, Peter was refocused. Each time Peter stated that he loved the Lord, Jesus gave him a command of some work he was to do. When Peter asked about the other disciples, Jesus redirected him back to his own life and what he had been called to do.

So where is the bow for my story? Sitting in that final class, I recalled how the desert cactus produces a crowning flower after months of quiet waiting. Like the cactus, I have waited; everything is done except for the bow.

And then I heard the small voice: "This is your ending as well as your new beginning. I, the Lord, have refilled you. I have provided for you physically, emotionally, and spiritually. I have sent many to teach you more of Me. I have refilled your life with living water and the Bread of Life. As we have spent time together, you, Jami, have been refilled with My love, my Spirit, and My peace.

"After your time of refilling, I have restored you by providing a new ministry for the coming year. Your business failure did not render you useless to My service. I will and am using you again. Start with the small step of being a discussion leader for next year's Bible Study Fellowship. Make the commitment to the extra time and study. Bring others alongside of you as you learn. You do have value to Me, my child. As you step out, filled anew with My love and power, you now know that you can and will be used again by Me for My purpose and glory.

"You now need to refocus your life. Take your eyes completely off of you. Do not compare your life with anyone else's life. I have a unique plan just for you, a plan to give you a future and a hope as you seek Me with all of your heart. My plan may or may not involve anything that you are doing right now. But be ready, for the time is short and the harvest is plenty. Whom shall I send?"

With the voice of the Lord sounding in my heart, I raised my hand and humbly whispered, "Lord, send me."

Afterword

After reading my manuscript, someone commented how great it was that God was changing my life on a daily basis and how knowing that would make it so much easier to get through it. I want to assure you that as I walked through my wilderness journey, I could not see God changing my life on a daily basis. It did not feel like I was making any progress on any front.

It has only been since 2009 that I have begun to understand that God was moving in my life and that I might be headed in a different direction. It took until October 2009 for that realization to really gel. I guess it is generally easier to see God's hand when looking backward rather than forward. I will admit, though, I never thought that He had left me, even though at times I was afraid, panicked, and worried.

So the point of the story is, no matter what you are facing, God is with you. No matter what your circumstances look like, remember that "we live by faith, not by sight" (2 Cor. 5:7). Our feelings most often are not truth, so we cannot trust them. However, God is truth.

As you walk through your own wilderness journey, immerse yourself in God by reading His Word, the Bible. Listen to uplifting praise music, and by all means, pray. No matter the words you choose, just talk to Him. He is listening, and He cares about the smallest detail of your life.

I would also encourage you to try an extended time of drawing nearer and closer to God. You do not have to quit your job in order to do this, but change your priorities for a period of time and ask God to come near to you. It is amazing what He will do.

I struggled with releasing this book to the public. I felt vulnerable and transparent. What would people think? How would they take it? Would I embarrass my family or myself? Would my clients lose confidence in me as their representative in a real estate transaction, knowing about all the foreclosures? After much prayer, I decided that the readers would realize that the message of my book is not about me, but about what God does in our lives: His faithfulness, His deliverance, and His provision. Thus the focus is on the message, and the message must be told.

Back to my original thought, so many months ago, that all of this was not for me alone. Mine is just one story of God's handiwork. Lord, may Your name be glorified and honored by my words.

"Praise be to the God and Father of our Lord
Jesus Christ, the Father of compassion and
the God of all comfort, who comforts us in
all our troubles, so that we can comfort those

*in any trouble with the comfort we ourselves
have received from God"* (2 Cor. 1:3–4).

Rebuilding Your Credit

I know how important a good FICO score is in our society. However, like me, many people who are facing the same financial hardship I endured have damaged their scores. I want to therefore share some practical tips on how to restore your credit score, and I want to make sure you understand how it is generated. Listed below is important information from the website MyFICO.com.

What's in Your FICO Score?

FICO scores are calculated from a lot of different credit data in your credit report. This data can be grouped into five categories as outlined below.

Payment history= 35%
Amounts owed= 30%
Length of credit history= 15%
New credit= 10%
Types of credit used= 10%

These percentages are based on the importance of the five categories for the general population. For particular groups—for example, people who have not been using credit long—the importance of these categories may be somewhat different.

Payment History

- Account payment information on specific types of accounts (credit cards, retail accounts, installment loans, finance company accounts, mortgages, etc.)
- Presence of adverse public records (bankruptcy, judgments, suits, liens, wage attachments, etc.), collection items, and/or delinquency (past-due items)
- Severity of delinquency (how long past due)
- Amount past due on delinquent accounts or collection items
- Time since past-due items (delinquency), adverse public records (if any), or collection items (if any)
- Number of past-due items on file
- Number of accounts paid as agreed

Amounts Owed

- Amount owed on accounts
- Amount owed on specific types of accounts
- Proportion of credit lines used (proportion of balances to total credit limits on certain types of revolving accounts)

- Proportion of installment loan amounts still owed (proportion of balance to original loan amount on certain types of installment loans)

Length of Credit History

- Time since accounts opened
- Time since account activity

New Credit

- Number of recently opened accounts
- Number of recent credit inquiries
- Time since recent account opening(s), by type of account
- Reestablishment of positive credit history following past payment problems

Please note the following:

- **A FICO score takes into consideration all these categories of information, not just one or two.**
  No one piece of information or one factor alone will determine your score.
- **The importance of any one factor depends on the overall information in your credit report.**
  For some people, a given factor may be more important than for someone else with a different credit history. In addition, as the information in your credit report changes, so does the importance of any one factor in deter-

mining your FICO score. Thus it's impossible to say exactly how important any single factor is in determining your score; even the levels of importance shown here are for the general population and will be different for different credit profiles. What's important is the mix of information, which varies from person to person and for any one person over time.

- **Your FICO score only looks at information in your credit report.**

  However, lenders look at many things when making a credit decision, including your income, how long you have worked at your present job, and the kind of credit you are requesting.

- **Your score considers both positive and negative information in your credit report.**

  Late payments will lower your score, but establishing or reestablishing a good track record of making payments on time will raise your FICO credit score.

Improving Your FICO Credit Score

It's important to note that raising your FICO credit score is a bit like losing weight: it takes time, and there is no quick fix. In fact, quick-fix efforts can backfire. The best advice is to manage credit responsibly over time by just following these tips and thus raising your credit score.

Tips on Payment History

- **Pay your bills on time!**
  Delinquent payments and collections can have a major negative impact on your FICO score.
- **If you have missed payments, get current and stay current.**
  The longer you pay your bills on time, the better your credit score.
- **Be aware that paying off a collection account will not remove it from your credit report.**
  It will stay on your report for seven years unless you request its removal which you can do.
- **If you are having trouble making ends meet, contact your creditors or see a legitimate credit counselor.**
  This won't improve your credit score immediately, but if you can begin to manage your credit and pay on time, your score will get better over time.

Tips on Amounts Owed

- **Keep balances low on credit cards and other forms of revolving credit.**
  Less than 50 percent of the available balance should be used at any given time.
- **Pay off debt rather than moving it around.**
  The most effective way to improve your credit score in this area is by paying down your

revolving credit. In fact, owing the same amount but having fewer open accounts may lower your score.

- **Don't close unused credit cards as a short-term strategy to raise your score.**
- **Don't open a number of new credit cards that you don't need just to increase your available credit.**

This approach could backfire and actually lower your credit score.

Tips on Length of Credit History

- **If you have been managing credit for only a short time, don't open too many new accounts too rapidly.**

New accounts will lower your average account age, which will have a larger effect on your score if you don't have much additional credit information. Also, rapid account buildup can look risky if you are a new credit user.

Tips on New Credit

- **Do your rate shopping for a given loan within a focused period of time.**

FICO scores distinguish between a search for a single loan and a search for many new credit lines in part by the length of time over which inquiries occur.

- **Reestablish your credit history if you have had problems.**

Opening new accounts responsibly and paying them off on time will raise your credit score in the long term.

- **It's okay to request and check your own credit report.**

This won't affect your score, as long as you order your credit report directly from the credit-reporting agency or through an organization authorized to provide credit reports to consumers.

Tips on Types of Credit Use

- **Apply for and open new credit accounts only as needed.**

Don't open accounts just to have a better credit mix; it probably won't raise your credit score.

- **Have credit cards, but manage them responsibly.**

In general, having credit cards and installment loans (and paying timely payments) will raise your credit score. Someone with no credit cards, for example, tends to be regarded as a higher risk than someone who has managed credit cards responsibly.

- **Note that closing an account doesn't make it go away.**

A closed account will still show up on your credit report and may be considered in calculating the score.

If you have a foreclosure on your record but previously had good credit, there are some things you can do to improve your FICO score. Here are some very practical tips given to me from a lender:

- **After a foreclosure or short sale, establish a new line of credit, even if you have to get a secured credit card.**

    A secured credit card is one in which you give the bank a thousand dollars and they give you a credit card for the same amount. Don't worry about the interest rate or the available balance. You are going to use this card to rebuild your credit.

- **Start using the card, but do not exceed 35-50 percent of the available balance, and do not pay it off every month.**

    Yes, you heard me correctly, and yes, it is counterintuitive to what you think you should do. However, using credit in a responsible way will help to raise your credit score. In the eyes of the credit card companies, paying the balance off every month does not reflect that you can use credit wisely, so do not pay it off. I suggest using the card for your gas purchases then pay the balance down to twenty dollars.

- **Then do it again next month.**

    Over time you will build up a record of responsible, wise use of credit.

Jesus, Your Personal Savior

When I think of how much I struggled as I walked through that difficult time in my life, I cannot imagine how others make it through difficult seasons in their lives without knowing God as their personal Savior. If you do not know Jesus Christ as your Lord and Savior, this chapter is for you.

"Steps of Peace with God" by Billy Graham Evangelistic Association

Do you understand God's plan of salvation? There are certain points we all need to understand about the heart of the Good News of Christ.

First, we all are sinners and stand under the judgment of God: "For all have sinned and fall short of the glory of God" (Rom. 3:23). We might believe that we are good enough to win God's favor or that we can perform certain religious acts to counterbalance our bad deeds, but the Bible states that we are all condemned, for "there is no one righteous, not even one" (Rom. 3:10).

Second, we need to understand what Christ has done to make our salvation possible. God loves us, and Christ came to make forgiveness and salvation possible. What did He do? He died on the cross as the complete sacrifice for our sins. He took upon Himself the judgment that we deserve.

Third, we need to respond to God's work. God in His grace offers us the gift of eternal life. But like any gift, it becomes ours only when we take it.

As part of this process, we must repent of our sins. Repentance carries with it the idea of confession, sorrow, turning, and changing. We cannot ask forgiveness over and over again for our sins and then return to those sins, expecting God to forgive us. We must turn from our practice of sin as best we know how and turn by faith to Christ as our Lord and Savior.

"It is by grace you have been saved, through faith—and this not from yourselves, it is the gift of God—not by works, so that no one can boast" (Eph. 2:8–9). Christ invites us to come to Him, and God has promised, "to all who received him, to those who believed in his name, he gave the right to become children of God" (John 1:12).

Fourth, we must understand the cost of coming to Christ and following Him. Jesus constantly called upon those who would follow Him to count the cost. A person must determine to leave his sins behind and turn from them, and some people may be unwilling to do so. There may be other costs as well when we decide to follow Christ. In some cultures, a person who turns to Christ may be disowned by family, alienated from social life, imprisoned, or even killed.

The ultimate cost of true discipleship is the cost of renouncing self: self-will, self-plans, self-motivations. Christ is to be Lord of our lives. Jesus declared, "If anyone would come after me, he must deny himself and take up his cross daily and follow me" (Luke 9:23). Jesus does not call us to a life of selfish comfort and ease—He calls us to battle! He calls us to give up our own plans and to follow Him without reserve—even to death.

Yes, it costs to follow Christ. It cost the apostle Paul the prestige of a high-level position in the Jewish nation. But he declared, "Whatever was to my profit I now consider loss for the sake of Christ. What is more, I consider everything a loss compared to the surpassing greatness of knowing Christ Jesus my Lord, for whose sake I have lost all things" (Phil. 3:7–8). Christ calls men and women to not only trust Him as Savior, but to also follow Him as Lord.

Fifth, salvation is intimately linked to the cross. The man who hung there between two thieves was without sin. His virgin birth by the miraculous intervention of the Holy Spirit meant that He did not inherit a sinful human nature. Neither did He commit any sin during His lifetime. Mary gave birth to the only perfect child, and He became the only perfect man. As such, He was uniquely qualified to put into action God's plan of salvation for mankind.

Why was Calvary's cross so special, so different from hundreds of other crosses used for Roman executions? It was because on that cross, Jesus suffered the punishment for sin that we all deserve. He was our substitute. He suffered the judgment and condemnation of death that our sinful nature and deeds deserve. "God made him who had no sin to be sin for us, so that in him we might become the righteousness of God" (2 Cor. 5:21).

Paul wrote to the church at Corinth, "I resolved to know nothing while I was with you except Jesus Christ and him crucified" (1 Cor. 2:2). Paul knew there was a built-in power in the cross and the resurrection.

Finally, faith is essential for salvation. But we must be absolutely clear on what we mean when we speak of salvation by faith. There are various kinds of belief or faith, and not all are linked to salvation. In the New Testament, faith means more than intellectual belief. It involves trust and commitment. You may say that you believe a bridge will hold your weight, but you really believe it only when you commit yourself to it and walk across it.

In the same way, saving faith involves an act of commitment and trust in which you commit your life to Jesus Christ and trust Him alone as your Savior and Lord. It is a personal and individual decision. It is more than assent to the historical or theological truth found in God's Word. It is faith in the promises of God that all who trust in Christ will not perish but will have eternal life. That is truly good news!

How to Receive Christ

I hope this information has helped you to understand what Jesus Christ has done to save us and what our response must be. If you are not sure that you are right with God, you can be sure—right now.

Remember, we must admit that we are sinners. We must turn away from our sins and turn to Christ. We must trust Him as our Savior and follow Him as our Lord. God promises that when we do this, He will save us and make us His children, and we will live with Him forever.

Step 1: GOD'S PURPOSE: PEACE AND LIFE

God loves you and wants you to experience peace and life—abundant and eternal.

The Bible says ...

"We have peace with God through our Lord Jesus Christ" (Rom. 5:1).

"For God so loved the world that He gave His only begotten Son, that whoever believes in Him should not perish but have everlasting life" John 3:16).

"I have come that they may have life, and that they may have it more abundantly" (John 10:10).

Why don't most people have this peace and abundant life that God planned for us to have?

Step 2: THE PROBLEM: OUR SEPARATION

God created us in His own image to have an abundant life. He did not make us like robots that had to automatically love and obey Him. God gave each of

179

us a free will and freedom of choice. We have chosen to disobey God and go our own willful way. We still make this choice today. This results in separation from God.

The Bible says . . .

"For all have sinned and fall short of the glory of God" (Rom. 3:23).

"For the wages of sin is death, but the gift of God is eternal life in Christ Jesus our Lord" (Rom. 6:23).

Our Attempts to Reach God

People have tried in many ways to bridge this gap between them and God.

The Bible says . . .

"There is a way that seems right to a man, but in the end it leads to death" (Prov. 14:12).

"But your iniquities have separated you from your God; your sins have hidden his face from you, so that he will not hear" (Isa. 59:2).

Step 3: GOD'S BRIDGE: THE CROSS

Jesus Christ died on the cross and rose from the grave. He paid the penalty for our sin and bridged the gap between God and people.

The Bible says . . .

"For there is one God and one mediator between God and men, the man Jesus Christ" (1 Tim. 2:5).

"For Christ died for sins once for all, the righteous for the unrighteous, to bring you to God" (1 Pet. 3:18).

"But God demonstrates his own love for us in this: While we were still sinners, Christ died for us" (Rom. 5:8).

God has provided the only way. Each person must make a choice.

Step 4: OUR RESPONSE: RECEIVE CHRIST

We must trust Jesus Christ as Lord and Savior and receive Him by personal invitation.

The Bible says . . .

"Here I am! I stand at the door and knock. If anyone hears my voice and opens the door, I will come in and eat with him, and he with me" (Rev. 3:20).

"Yet to all who received him, to those who believed in his name, he gave the right to become children of God" (John 1:12).

"That if you confess with your mouth, 'Jesus is Lord,' and believe in your heart that God raised him from the dead, you will be saved" (Rom. 10:9).

Where Are You?

Will you receive Jesus Christ right now? Here is how you can receive Him:

1. Admit your need. (I am a sinner.)
2. Be willing to turn from your sins. (Repent.)
3. Believe that Jesus Christ died for you on the cross and rose from the grave.
4. Through prayer, invite Jesus Christ to come in and control your life through the Holy Spirit. (Receive Him as Lord and Savior.)

How to Pray:

Dear Lord Jesus, I know that I am a sinner and need Your forgiveness. I believe that You died for my sins. I want to turn from my sins. I now invite You to come into my heart and life. I want to trust and follow You as Lord and Savior. In Jesus' name I pray. Amen.

God's Assurance: His Word

If you prayed this prayer, look at what happened!

The Bible says . . .

"Everyone who calls on the name of the Lord will be saved" (Rom. 10:13).

Did you sincerely ask Jesus Christ to come into your life? Where is He right now? What has He given you?

"For it is by grace you have been saved, through faith—and this not from yourselves, it is the gift of God—not by works, so that no one can boast" (Eph. 2:8–9).

Upon receiving Christ, you are born into God's family through the supernatural work of the Holy Spirit, who indwells every believer. This is called regeneration, or the "new birth."

This is just the beginning of your wonderful new life in Christ. To deepen this relationship, you should do the following:

1. Read your Bible every day to know Christ better.
2. Talk to God in prayer every day.
3. Tell others about Christ.
4. Worship, fellowship, and serve with other Christians in a church where Christ is preached.
5. As Christ's representative in a needy world, demonstrate your new life by your love and concern for others.

NOTES

[1] Ty Lacy, "You'll Get Through This," Copyright © 1996, Ariose Music (ASCAP). Administered at EMICMGPublishing.com, 2000. All rights reserved. Used by permission; license #510339.

[2] Randall, Stacy, I Was There, 2001

[3] Ben Glover and Ronnie Freeman, "Love Won't Leave You Now," Copyright © 2000, Randy Cox Music. Administered by Brentwood-Benson Music Publishing. All rights reserved. Used by permission; license #432557.

[4] Bruce Wilkinson, *The Prayer of Jabez* (Sister, OR: Multnomah Publishers, Inc., 2000).

[5] HOLY BIBLE, NEW INTERNATIONAL VERSION ®. Life Application Study Bible. COPYRIGHT © 1973,1978, 1984 by International Bible Society. Used by permission of Zonderdervan Publishing House. All rights reserved.

VI Andrae Crouch, "Through it All," Manna Music, © 1971.

VII Dutch Sheets, *Authority in Prayer* (Minneapolis, MN: Bethany House, 2006).

VIII Sam Mizell/Arron Rice, "Jesus Calling," Copyright Emack Music Rizzle Music/Unknown publisher. All rights reserved. Used by permission; license #432556.

CPSIA information can be obtained at www.ICGtesting.com

263268BV00005B/3/P

9 781613 790649